MEDICAL SPANISH FOR HEALTHCARE HEROES

A COMPREHENSIVE GUIDE TO QUICKLY MASTER
VITAL TERMINOLOGY, EXPERTLY NAVIGATE MEDICAL
INTERACTIONS AND DELIVER SUPERIOR PATIENT
CARE IN 31 DAYS!

SOL MANCILLA

CONTENTS

INTRODUCTION

The more I understood the patient's story, the more I realized that it was not just the disease that was important; it was the patient's story that needed to be understood.

— BERNARD LOWN

Picture this: Within the bustling environment of a hospital, a dedicated healthcare professional stands at the bedside of a patient. In this critical moment, they share more than just a room; they share an unspoken connection built on trust and understanding. This connection transcends mere medical knowledge—it's about empathy, reassurance, and effective communication. Yet, in this scenario, there's a challenging obstacle, a barrier that often separates this profound connection: a language barrier. The patient, speaking Spanish, yearns for comfort and clarity, while the healthcare professional strives to provide the best care possible, hindered by linguistic limitations. This is not just a hypothetical scene; it's a reality faced by countless healthcare heroes every day.

You may agree with me on something: Communication is not a trivial skill; it allows people to establish and strengthen conventions, bonds, and agreements on which our entire social dynamic and our civilization are built.

In a medical context, communication goes beyond symbols: It's a lifeline, a conduit through which expertise and compassion flow. Language barriers are undesirable challenges in this context. If the patient is not able to properly communicate their affairs to the medical professional and vice versa, the consequences are profound. The need for effective transmission in healthcare, especially in culturally diverse societies, is not a matter of mere convenience; it's an imperative.

Consider this startling fact: Spanish is the second most spoken language in the United States, with over 40 million native speakers and millions more who are bilingual (Thompson, 2021). Yet, a significant portion of healthcare professionals find themselves navigating the complex topography of patient care without the linguistic tools required to provide optimal care to Spanish-speaking patients. This discrepancy leads to misunderstandings, misdiagnoses, and a profound lack of trust in the healthcare system, and ultimately can potentially affect people's health and well-being. It's a challenge that has far-reaching implications, touching the lives of countless individuals who seek healthcare.

Allow me to introduce myself. I am an advocate for communication. I am just an observer of the healthcare system who believes unequivocally in the power and importance of human communication. Through my own experience and that of people in my surroundings, I have noticed the frustrations and limitations that healthcare professionals face when they cannot effectively communicate with their patients.

In many cases within this sector, healthcare professionals work alongside interpreters to bridge the language gap between them and their patients. While this approach ensures understanding, there is immense value in healthcare providers being able to communicate directly with their patients and their families. The ability to speak in Spanish empowers nurses, doctors, and other professionals, instilling a sense of competence and fostering a deeper and more human connection with those in their care.

As a bilingual native Spanish speaker with a career in communication, I have dedicated my life to finding solutions to different challenges related to language barriers. I understand the significance of compassionate care, and I firmly believe that language should never impede it. That's why I am writing this book—to empower healthcare professionals like you with the tools to break down language barriers, foster understanding, and provide the highest level of care to every patient, regardless of the language they speak.

This book possesses a clear and unwavering purpose: to boost healthcare professionals' communication skills and to help them learn Spanish not merely as a language but as an indispensable means of enhancing the quality of care they offer to Spanish-speaking patients. It is about bridging the gap between the mastery of medical terminology and the ability to engage in meaningful conversations with patients, their families, and the broader community.

These pages are more than just a language guide; they contain a comprehensive resource that is meticulously crafted to transform healthcare professionals into confident and effective communicators in Spanish.

This guide is divided into seven chapters, each thoughtfully structured to provide you with the knowledge and skills necessary for success.

Throughout the book, you will find pronunciation guides and phonetic support to ensure that your spoken Spanish is clear and confident. The content is structured for easy navigation, and practical exercises make learning engaging and effective.

I extend an invitation to venture on this exceptional trip to learn Spanish for healthcare. Irrespective of your current level of Spanish proficiency, this book will equip you with tools to enhance your communication with Spanish-speaking patients. It will empower you in your healthcare career, enabling you to provide compassionate, efficient care to a broader and more diverse patient population.

As you turn the pages of this book, you take the first deliberate step towards breaking down language barriers in healthcare. I ask you to seize this opportunity, to dive into the first chapter, and to commit wholeheartedly to becoming a healthcare hero who communicates with efficacy, empathizes profoundly, and cares comprehensively.

Turn the page; your journey commences now. *¡Adelante!*

BUILDING THE BRIDGE: BASICS OF SPANISH FOR HEALTHCARE

F or healthcare professionals, effective communication is a —literally—vital skill. The ability to convey critical information, understand patients' needs, and provide clear instructions can be a matter of life and death. Now, imagine encountering a patient who speaks Spanish as their primary language, and you, as a healthcare professional, find yourself grappling with the language barrier. This is where our journey begins.

This first chapter is your launching pad into the realm of Spanish for healthcare. I admit that you have a demanding profession, with little time to spare for elaborate language courses. That's why this whole book is designed to be precise, focused, and tailored to the unique demands of your field.

Through the following pages, we will lay the foundation of your Spanish language skills, equipping you with the rudimentary grammar, critical vocabulary, and correct pronunciation necessary to navigate healthcare contexts with confidence and competence.

We'll start with the understanding that Spanish is a doorway to deeper, more human connections with your patients. It's about building trust, ensuring accurate diagnoses, and delivering care with empathy. You are now embarking on a journey to break down language barriers, provide superior care to Spanish-speaking patients, and enhance your professional profile in the healthcare domain.

¡Comencemos!

MORE THAN JUST A LANGUAGE

With approximately 460 million native speakers, Spanish holds the distinguished title of being the second most spoken language in the world, trailing only behind Mandarin Chinese (McCarthy, 2020). It's a testament to the rich diversity of cultures and communities it connects. Yet, its significance in the healthcare landscape extends far beyond sheer numbers.

Let's zoom in on the United States, where the Spanish language finds a thriving home. According to the Instituto Cervantes (Martinez, 2015), a renowned institution dedicated to the Spanish language and culture, the United States boasts the second-highest concentration of Spanish speakers on the planet, surpassed only by Mexico. This fact paints a compelling picture: A substantial portion of patients navigating the American healthcare system converse primarily in Spanish. This demographic reality serves as a poignant reminder of the importance of Spanish proficiency for healthcare professionals.

However, the essence of learning this beautiful language in the healthcare arena goes beyond a mere statistical imperative. It's a journey that transcends numbers and charts, aiming to bridge a profound communication gap. Think of it this way: Learning Spanish isn't just about adding a language skill to your resume; it's about dismantling barriers that separate patients from their caregivers.

Consider the role of interpreters, those professionals who facilitate communication between patients and healthcare providers. While their assistance is undeniably practical, it can inadvertently create a sense of automation and detachment in the patient–professional relationship. Conversations become transactional, as clinical information is relayed through an intermediary.

Now, imagine the transformation that occurs when healthcare professionals can converse directly with their patients in their native language. It's like opening a window into their world, allowing you to connect on a deeper level. It's not just about relaying medical information; it's about forging a connection built on empathy, understanding, and trust. It's about giving autonomy to healthcare professionals in the field to engage in meaningful conversations that transcend clinical verbiage.

As a healthcare professional, your commitment to patient care extends beyond the clinical aspects. It encompasses the emotional and psychological well-being of your patients. The ability to converse with them in their preferred language is a powerful gesture of respect, a demonstration of empathy, and a catalyst for building trust. It empowers you to truly understand your patients' needs, fears, and aspirations, leading to more effective diagnoses and treatments.

The pages that follow will equip you with the tools and knowledge needed to bridge this language intermission and elevate your healthcare practice to new heights.

BASIC SPANISH GRAMMAR

One of the key characteristics that set Spanish apart is its phonetic nature. It means that words are pronounced precisely as they are written. Unlike some other languages where pronunciation can be a labyrinth of exceptions, in Spanish, what you see is what you say. This phonetic quality lends a sense of predictability and consistency to the language, making it more approachable for learners.

Now, let's bridge this language knowledge to your healthcare practice. Imagine being able to construct simple sentences in Spanish. It's akin to unlocking a treasure trove of understanding when it comes to your patient's symptoms and medical procedures. The ability to communicate basic concepts can be a game-changer in patient interactions.

For instance, consider the significance of being able to ask a simple question like *¿Dónde le duele?* (Where does it hurt?). This straightforward inquiry can provide invaluable insights into a patient's condition, enabling you to pinpoint the source of discomfort and take swift action.

Likewise, the power of being able to make statements such as *Necesito tomar su presión arterial* (I need to take your blood pressure) should not be underestimated. This concise sentence not only conveys your intention but also reassures the patient by keeping them informed about the procedure. It's a bridge between medical expertise and patient understanding.

These examples illustrate how even a basic grasp of Spanish grammar can significantly enhance patient interactions in healthcare settings. It's about breaking down the language barrier, one sentence at a time, and forging connections that transcend linguistic differences. In the subsequent sections of this chapter, we will delve deeper into the foundations of Spanish grammar, equipping you with the tools to construct meaningful sentences and engage in more effective patient communication.

Let's dive into the foundations of Spanish grammar one by one.

Subject Pronouns

Subject pronouns are essential elements in constructing sentences as they indicate who or what is performing the action of the verb. Here are the Spanish subject pronouns along with their English translations:

Subject pronouns (*pronombres personales*)	English translation
Yo	I
Tú	You: informal singular
Él / Ella	He / She
Usted	You: formal singular
Nosotros / Nosotras	We
Vosotros / Vosotras	You all: informal plural
Ellos (masculine) / Ellas (feminine)	They
Ustedes	You all: formal plural

Examples:

- *Yo hablo español* (I speak Spanish)
- *Tú estudias medicina* (You study medicine)
- *Él es el médico* (He is the doctor)
- *Nosotros trabajamos en el hospital* (We work at the hospital)

Masculine and Feminine Nouns

In Spanish, nouns have gender, which can be masculine (*masculino*) or feminine (*femenino*). Additionally, articles must match the gender and number of nouns. Here's a chart with some examples:

Gender	Noun	Article	English translation
Masculine	El chico	El (The)	The boy
	El hospital	El (The)	The hospital
	Los libros	Los (The)	The books
	Los estudiantes	Los (The)	The students
Feminine	La chica	La (The)	The girl
	La enfermera	La (The)	The nurse
	Las flores	Las (The)	The flowers
	Las amigas	Las (The)	The friends (all female)

Verb Conjugations

Spanish verbs undergo conjugation to match the subject of the sentence in terms of person and number. Let's examine the present simple, past simple, and future simple tenses, using the basic verbs *ser, estar, and tener.*

In the following chart, you'll find the conjugation in the **present simple** tense for the verbs *ser* (to be), *estar* (to be), and *tener* (to have).

Ser (to be [for permanent states]):

Subject pronouns	Conjugation	English translation
Yo	*soy*	I am
Tú	*eres*	You are (informal singular)
Él / Ella / Usted	*es*	He / She / You (formal) is/are
Nosotros / Nosotras	*somos*	We are
Vosotros / Vosotras	*sois*	You all are (informal plural)
Ellos / Ellas / Ustedes	*son*	They / You all (formal) are

Estar (to be [for temporary states]):

Subject pronouns	Conjugation	English translation
Yo	*estoy*	I am
Tú	*estás*	You are (informal singular)
Él / Ella / Usted	*está*	He / She / You (formal) is/are
Nosotros / Nosotras	*estamos*	We are
Vosotros / Vosotras	*estáis*	You all are (informal plural)
Ellos / Ellas / Ustedes	*están*	They / You all (formal) are

Tener (to have):

Subject pronouns	Conjugation	English translation
Yo	tengo	I have
Tú	tienes	You have (informal singular)
Él / Ella / Usted	tiene	He / She / You (formal) has/ have
Nosotros / Nosotras	tenemos	We have
Vosotros / Vosotras	tenéis	You all have (informal plural)
Ellos / Ellas / Ustedes	tienen	They / You all (formal) have

Now, let's take a look at the conjugation for these verbs in the **past simple** form.

Ser (to be):

Subject pronouns	Conjugation	English translation
Yo	fui	I was
Tú	fuiste	You were (informal singular)
Él / Ella / Usted	fue	He / She / You (formal) was/ were
Nosotros / Nosotras	fuimos	We were
Vosotros / Vosotras	fuisteis	You all were (informal plural)
Ellos / Ellas / Ustedes	fueron	They / You all (formal) were

Estar (to be):

Subject pronouns	Conjugation	English translation
Yo	estuve	I was
Tú	estuviste	You were (informal singular)
Él / Ella / Usted	estuvo	He / She / You (formal) was/were
Nosotros / Nosotras	estuvimos	We were
Vosotros / Vosotras	estuvisteis	You all were (informal plural)
Ellos / Ellas / Ustedes	estuvieron	They / You all (formal) were

Tener (to have):

Subject pronouns	Conjugation	English translation
Yo	tuve	I had
Tú	tuviste	You had (informal singular)
Él / Ella / Usted	tuvo	He / She / You (formal) had
Nosotros / Nosotras	tuvimos	We had
Vosotros / Vosotras	tuvisteis	You all had (informal plural)
Ellos / Ellas / Ustedes	tuvieron	They / You all (formal) had

For **future simple:**

Ser (to be):

Subject pronouns	Conjugation	English translation
Yo	seré	I will be
Tú	serás	You will be (informal singular)
Él / Ella / Usted	será	He / She / You (formal) will be
Nosotros / Nosotras	seremos	We will be
Vosotros / Vosotras	seréis	You all will be (informal plural)
Ellos / Ellas / Ustedes	serán	They / You all (formal) will be

Estar (to be):

Subject pronouns	Conjugation	English translation
Yo	estaré	I will be
Tú	estarás	You will be (informal singular)
Él / Ella / Usted	estará	He / She / You (formal) will be
Nosotros / Nosotras	estaremos	We will be
Vosotros / Vosotras	estaréis	You all will be (informal plural)
Ellos / Ellas / Ustedes	estarán	They / You all (formal) will be

Tener (to have):

Subject pronouns	Conjugation	English translation
Yo	tendré	I will have
Tú	tendrás	You will have (informal singular)
Él / Ella / Usted	tendrá	He / She / You (formal) will have
Nosotros / Nosotras	tendremos	We will have
Vosotros / Vosotras	tendréis	You all will have (informal plural)
Ellos / Ellas / Ustedes	tendrán	They / You all (formal) will have

Basic Sentence Structure

While Spanish and English share some similarities in sentence structure, there are also notable differences.

In both Spanish and English, the basic sentence structure follows the subject-verb-object (SVO) order, where

- **Subject (S)** refers to the person or thing performing the action.
- **Verb (V)** represents the action being performed.
- **Object (O)** is the receiver of the action.

Let me illustrate this similarity with the following example:

- *Ella (S) lee (V) un libro (O)* (She [S] reads [V] a book [O]). This sentence has SVO structure in both languages.

However, there are still myriad differences from the English structure:

- **Adjective placement:** In Spanish, adjectives typically follow the noun they describe. This is different from English, where adjectives often precede the noun. For example, in Spanish, you would say "Una flor hermosa" (A beautiful flower), where "*flor*" is the object and "*hermosa*" is the adjective.
- **Subject pronouns:** While English often includes subject pronouns (I, you, he, she, etc.) in sentences, Spanish can omit them because the verb conjugation already indicates the subject. For instance: While in English you say "I am a nurse," in Spanish, you could perfectly omit the pronoun since the verb is conjugated for its particular form. So you could rather say "*Yo soy enfermera*" or simply "*Soy enfermera.*"
- **Question formation:** In English, questions are often formed by inverting the subject and the auxiliary verb (e.g., "*Is* he coming?"). In Spanish, questions are typically formed by adding an interrogative sign at the beginning and end of the sentence, with no inversion required, since the difference between a question and an affirmation is given by the signs in writing and by the tone spoken. For example: "Are you a nurse?" translates to "*¿Eres enfermera?*" Without the interrogative signs and said with an affirmative tone, this same sentence becomes a statement: "*Eres enfermera*" (You are a nurse).
- **Double negatives**: While in English, double negatives are considered grammatically incorrect and cancel each

other out (e.g., "I don't know nothing"). In Spanish, double negatives are standard and intensify the negation. For example: "*No sé nada*" has two negative words and literally translates to "I don't know nothing," but the real meaning is more like "I know nothing."

- **Adjective agreement:** As we just learned, in Spanish, adjectives must agree in gender and number with the nouns they modify. This means that if the noun is masculine and singular, the adjective must also be masculine and singular. In English, adjectives do not change based on the gender or number of the noun. For example: "The tall doctor" translates to "*El médico alto*" (masculine) or "*La médica alta*" (feminine). Likewise, "The tall doctors" would equally translate to "*Los doctores altos*" or "*Las doctoras altas.*"

VOCABULARY: THE BUILDING BLOCKS OF COMMUNICATION

Learning the basic Spanish vocabulary is the foundation for efficient communication with Spanish-speaking patients. Within the healthcare context, being able to convey fundamental phrases and terms not only demonstrates respect but also fosters a sense of trust and rapport. Here are essential Spanish phrases and words you should know, along with their English translations:

- *Hola*: Hello
- *¿Cómo está?*: How are you?
- *Gracias*: Thank you

- *Por favor*: Please
- *De acuerdo*: Okay
- *Lo siento*: I'm sorry
- *Necesito su ayuda*: I need your help
- *Está bien*: It's okay
- *¿Qué pasa?*: What's happening?
- *¿Puede explicar más?*: Can you explain more?
- *Aquí estoy para ayudar*: I'm here to help

Beyond greetings and courteous expressions, healthcare professionals should familiarize themselves with basic medical terms, as they are essential for patient assessment and care. In the following chapters, we will delve deeper into specific vocabulary for each medical area. Meanwhile, here are some crucial medical vocabulary words in Spanish and their English translations:

1. *Dolor*: Pain
2. *Fiebre*: Fever
3. *Respiración*: Breathing
4. *Sangre*: Blood
5. *Presión arterial*: Blood pressure
6. *Medicamento*: Medication
7. *Enfermedad*: Illness
8. *Lesión*: Injury
9. *Cirugía*: Surgery
10. *Radiografía*: X-ray
11. *Laboratorio*: Laboratory
12. *Emergencia*: Emergency

As a healthcare professional aiming to enhance your Spanish language skills for effective patient communication, you have a plethora of resources at your fingertips to practice and improve your abilities. Beyond formal lessons and structured courses, there are several avenues you can explore to integrate Spanish into your daily life and continuously elevate your language proficiency.

One engaging option is **Spanish-language news**. Tuning into Spanish news broadcasts or reading Spanish news articles allows you to stay updated on healthcare developments while refining your language skills. This exposure often includes interviews with medical experts, offering a firsthand encounter with medical terminology and its practical applications.

Consider seeking out **language exchange partners** who are native Spanish speakers. Offering your English language skills in exchange for conversational Spanish practice can be highly beneficial. Websites and platforms like *Tandem* and *ConversationExchange* facilitate these language exchange partnerships, creating opportunities for mutual learning and cultural exchange.

YouTube can be an unexpected but effective teacher. There are numerous **tutorials** available, covering various aspects of the Spanish language, including medical terminology and pronunciation. Visual aids can be particularly helpful in understanding complex concepts and mastering pronunciation.

For those looking to dive deeper into professional terminology, exploring **medical journals and publications** in Spanish can be instructive. Reading articles and publications related to healthcare in Spanish enables you to immerse yourself in specialized vocabulary and stay informed about medical advancements in Spanish-speaking regions.

Engaging with online **language communities** dedicated to learning Spanish is another fruitful avenue. Joining forums or communities provides a supportive environment where you can ask questions, share experiences, and practice conversational skills. Platforms like Reddit's r/Spanish and language-learning websites often have active communities eager to assist learners like you.

While *Duolingo* is a popular starting point, there are other **language-learning apps** to explore, such as *Babbel*, *Memrise*, or *Rosetta Stone.* These apps often offer more comprehensive courses that focus on speaking and listening skills, which are crucial for effective communication with patients.

Seeking out **language meetup groups** in your local area can provide opportunities for in-person interactions and cultural immersion. These groups often gather for social events or language practice sessions, fostering an environment where you can comfortably practice your conversational skills.

Lastly, keep an eye out for **Spanish-language films and TV shows** with subtitles. Watching them can be an enjoyable way to improve your listening skills while familiarizing yourself with colloquial language and cultural nuances.

Before delving into pronunciation and other topics, let me tell you that Spanish grammar is one of the most complex and extensive in the linguistic world. Here, for practical reasons, I have summarized the bases and foundations of the grammar of this language as much as possible so that you as a health professional can learn what is fundamental and necessary to begin communicating effectively with your patients as soon as possible. Even so, if you are interested in continuing to delve deeper into the grammatical foundations of Spanish, I recommend that you read my other book, *Learn Spanish for Adult Beginners: Speak Confidently & Impress Your Amigos - A No-Nonsense Guide to Quickly Learn Vocabulary, Common Phrases, and Master Pronunciation* (Mancilla, 2023), where you can learn more extensively everything related to this wonderful language, including its culture, nuances and diversity.

PRONUNCIATION: THE KEY TO BEING UNDERSTOOD

The correct pronunciation is paramount when communicating in a healthcare setting, as it not only facilitates effective interaction but also helps prevent misunderstandings that could potentially compromise patient care.

In Spanish, pronunciation generally follows a set of straightforward rules, making it accessible for English speakers. However, there are certain nuances to be aware of, especially for healthcare professionals aiming for clear and accurate communication.

One of the notable characteristics of Spanish pronunciation is that the letter "h'" is **always silent**. Unlike in English, where "h" can significantly impact word pronunciation, in Spanish, it is merely a placeholder. For instance, the word "hospital" in Spanish is pronounced "os-pee-tal," with no "h" sound.

Another letter that may pose a challenge for English speakers is "j," which sounds like the English "h." This can be particularly noticeable in words like "jalapeño," where the "j" is pronounced like "ha-lah-pee-nyo."

The Spanish "r" can be a bit tricky for English speakers as well. Unlike the English "r," which is pronounced with a rolling or flapping motion of the tongue, the Spanish "r" is a single flap of the tongue against the roof of the mouth. It's a stronger and quicker sound. To practice this sound, you can try repeating words like "*perro*" (dog) or "*carro*" (car).

Another letter you must be aware of is the "ñ". This one is a unique character in the Spanish language and represents a distinct sound. It is pronounced much like the "ny" in the English word "canyon." Whether discussing conditions like "*niños*" (children) or medical terms like "*niñera*" (babysitter), mastering the pronunciation of the "ñ" is crucial for healthcare professionals to convey information accurately and build rapport with Spanish-speaking patients—and avoid sounding funny.

Additionally, Spanish vowels are relatively simple, with **each vowel having only one sound**. This contrasts with English, where vowel sounds can vary significantly depending on the word. For example, in Spanish, "a" always sounds like the "a" in "father," "e" like the "e" in "red," "i" like the "ee" in "feet," "o" like the "o" in "go," and "u" like the "u" in "blue."

To practice and improve pronunciation, healthcare professionals can explore various resources beyond textbooks. Websites like Forvo offer a vast collection of words and phrases pronounced by native speakers. This can be a valuable tool to listen and mimic correct pronunciation. Additionally, Google Translate's audio function can provide a quick way to hear the correct pronunciation of words or phrases, making it a handy resource in daily practice.

Throughout this book you will frequently find the pronunciation of Spanish words given by the SPA Hispanic phonetics protocol. The idea is that you pronounce each syllable with the sound that you as an English speaker intuitively associate with that nomenclature. For example, the pronunciation of the word "*fiebre*" (fever) is given by: fee-eh-breh.

Let's expand on our current vocabulary implementing the correct pronunciation for each word:

- *Jeringa* (syringe): heh-reen-gah
- *Vendaje* (bandage): ben-dah-heh
- *Termómetro* (thermometer): tehr-moh-meh-troh
- *Tos* (cough): tohs
- *Mareo* (dizziness): mah-reh-oh
- *Vómito* (vomit): voh-mee-toh
- *Diarrea* (diarrhea): dee-ah-reh-ah
- *Picazón* (itching): pee-kah-sohn
- *Sarpullido* (rash): sahr-poo-yee-doh
- *Fatiga* (fatigue): fah-tee-gah
- *Estreñimiento* (constipation): es-treh-nyee-mee-ehn-toh

- *Sangrado* (bleeding): sahn-grah-doh
- *Inyección* (injection): een-yehk-see-ohn
- *Muletas* (crutches): moo-leh-tahs
- *Curita* (band-aid): koo-ree-tah

PRACTICE MAKES PERFECT

Let's talk about practice because, when it comes to learning a new language, it's all about practice and repetition. As a healthcare professional, you already understand the value of practice in your field, and the same principle applies here.

So, how can you practice your Spanish in a way that complements your busy schedule? Well, first and foremost, consider speaking simple Spanish phrases with your Spanish-speaking colleagues or patients (with their consent, of course). Just like any skill, practice makes perfect, and engaging in real conversations, even if they're brief, can boost your confidence and fluency.

But what if you're looking for more flexible options? Watching Spanish TV shows or listening to Spanish podcasts is an excellent choice. *Grey's Anatomy* is available in Spanish on Netflix. Why not give it a shot? It's a fun way to immerse yourself in the language while enjoying a familiar storyline. Additionally, there are fantastic podcasts like *Notes in Spanish* specifically designed for Spanish learners. These resources offer valuable insights into the language and culture, and you can listen to them during your commute or while exercising.

Remember, it's all about finding opportunities to integrate Spanish into your daily life. The more you practice, the more comfortable and confident you'll become in using Spanish in your healthcare interactions. So, seize those chances and you'll soon see your language skills improve!

A STEP TOWARDS CAREER ENHANCEMENT

Did you know that the demand for bilingual workers in the US has more than doubled between 2010 and 2015 (Colon, 2019)? That's a significant shift in the job market, and it's not slowing down. Being bilingual, especially in Spanish, can give you a competitive edge in your healthcare career. It opens doors to new opportunities, whether you're seeking a better position, aiming for a leadership role, or simply looking to stand out in a crowded field.

But there's more to it than just job prospects. Learning Spanish can lead to better job satisfaction as well. When you can communicate effectively with a wider range of patients, you're not just providing medical assistance; you're offering empathy, understanding, and a sense of trust. These qualities can profoundly impact patient outcomes and your own sense of fulfillment in your profession.

On a personal sphere, learning Spanish—like any other language—is a gateway to the richness of foreign cultures and art. Delving into the Spanish language allows you to connect with the soul of these cultures, appreciate the nuances of their traditions, and understand the profound beauty of their art, literature, and history. From the vibrant rhythms of salsa music to the marvelous tales written by Gabriel García Marquez and José Saramago, the Hispanic world is a treasure trove of creativity and passion.

As you immerse yourself in this language, you'll discover the joy of connecting with people from diverse backgrounds, exploring new cuisines, and experiencing the warmth of Hispanic hospitality, enriching a journey that broadens your horizons, ignites your curiosity, and fills your life with a deeper appreciation for the beauty of our global community.

So, as we conclude this chapter, I want to invite you to continue this journey with us. In the chapters ahead, we'll delve deeper into the intricacies of the Spanish language, cultural nuances, and practical strategies for improving your language skills. Whether you're just starting or already have a foundation in Spanish, this book is here to support you on your path to becoming a more confident and capable healthcare professional.

Te veo del otro lado.

EXERCISES AND PRACTICE

A. Complete the following sentences by selecting the correct subject pronoun in Spanish:

1. _____ *soy enfermera.*
2. _____ *necesito su ayuda.*
3. _____ *está en el hospital.*
4. _____ *tienes fiebre.*

5. _____ *estamos aquí para cuidarte.*

Translation:

1. I am a nurse.
2. I need your help.
3. He is in the hospital.
4. You have a fever.
5. We are here to take care of you.

Answers:

1. *Yo*
2. *Yo*
3. *Él*
4. *Tu*
5. *Nosotros/as*

B. Complete the following charts with the corresponding words and articles:

Article	Word in Spanish	English translation
El	hospital	The hospital
____(1)	enfermera	The nurse (feminine)
Los	pacientes	_____(2) (masculine)
El	médico	The doctor (masculine)
La	medicina	The medicine
____(3)	tratamiento	The treatment
Los	síntomas	The symptoms
Las	_____(4)	The X-rays
El	diagnóstico	The diagnosis
____(5)	_____(6)	The prescription

Answers:

1. *La*
2. *The patients*
3. *El*
4. *Radiografías*
5. *La*
6. *Receta*

C. Translate the following sentences from English to Spanish, making sure to conjugate the verbs correctly according to the given tense and subject:

1. He helps the patient. (Present Simple):

   _____

2. They treated the injury. (Past Simple):

   _____

3. She explained the procedure. (Past Simple):

   _____

4. We are treating the illness. (Present Simple):

   _____

5. You will help the children. (Future Simple):

   _____

Answers:

1. *Él ayuda al paciente.*
2. *Ellos trataron la lesión.*
3. *Ella explicó el procedimiento.*
4. *Estamos tratando la enfermedad.*
5. *Tú ayudarás a los niños.*

D. Read the following medical terms and phrases in Spanish and repeat after the pronunciation guide to rehearse your pronunciation:

1. *Consulta médica* (kohn-sool-tah meh-dee-kah)
2. *Radiografía* (rah-dee-oh-grah-fee-ah)
3. *Enfermedad crónica* (ehn-fehr-meh-dahd kroh-nee-kah)
4. *Cirugía cardíaca* (see-roo-hee-ah kahr-dee-ah-kah)
5. *Tratamiento efectivo* (trah-tah-mee-ehn-toh eh-fehk-tee-boh)

Feel free to use online resources or language apps for correct pronunciation reference. These exercises will help you strengthen your foundational Spanish skills for healthcare communication. Enjoy practicing!

2

MEDICAL SPANISH DICTIONARY: A HEALTHCARE PROFESSIONAL'S GUIDE

N ow that you know the basics of Spanish grammar, you can begin to construct simple sentences. But before you can communicate with your patients and other Spanish speakers in the medical environment, you need to learn the terminology of the clinical field. We will dedicate the following pages to this.

This comprehensive guide offers not only translations of essential medical terms into Spanish but also provides pronunciation guides and examples of contextual usage. Whether you are a nurse, doctor, or any healthcare professional, this chapter aims to equip you with the linguistic tools necessary to communicate effectively with Spanish-speaking patients.

Vamos al lío.

GLOSSARY OF GENERAL HEALTH TERMS

General health terms serve as the foundation of any clear medical conversation. As healthcare professionals, you understand better than anyone the importance of precise and clear communication when discussing health-related matters with patients and their families. This section of our Medical Spanish Dictionary equips you with the fundamental vocabulary necessary for effective communication.

For instance, terms like "*salud*" (health), "*enfermedad*" (disease), and "*tratamiento*" (treatment) may seem basic. Still, they are the building blocks of understanding and conveying crucial information regarding a patient's well-being.

The knowledge of these terms allows you to grasp and convey information about a patient's health condition accurately. When a patient mentions "*salud*" or "*enfermedad*," you will immediately recognize that they are discussing their health or disease. For instance, if a patient says, "*Tengo una enfermedad del corazón*," you will readily understand that they have a heart disease.

However, it's not just about knowing these terms; correct pronunciation is equally necessary. For example, the word "*salud*" is pronounced as "sah-lood" in Spanish. Precise pronunciation is your key to preventing misunderstandings and ensuring that your patient interactions are as effective and compassionate as possible. So, let's delve into these essential terms, master their pronunciation, and empower you to navigate medical conversations with confidence and precision.

ANATOMY IN SPANISH: NAMING THE BODY PARTS

Let's start with the basics: the body parts. In the following table, you can find the most common limbs and body parts.

External body parts (*partes externas del cuerpo*):

Body part	Pronunciation	English translation
Cabeza	kah-beh-zah	Head
Cara	kah-rah	Face
Ojos	oh-hohs	Eyes
Oídos	oh-ee-dohs	Ears
Nariz	nah-reez	Nose
Boca	boh-kah	Mouth
Dientes	dee-ehn-tehs	Teeth
Cuello	kuh-eh-yoh	Neck
Hombros	ohm-brohs	Shoulders
Pecho	peh-choh	Chest
Espalda	ehs-pahl-dah	Back
Brazos	brah-zohs	Arms
Codos	coh-dohs	Elbows
Manos	mah-nohs	Hands
Dedos	dhe-dohs	Fingers
Vientre	bee-ehn-treh	Belly
Caderas	kah-deh-rahs	Hips
Piernas	pee-ehr-nahs	Legs

Rodillas	roh-dee-yahs	Knees
Pies	pee-ehs	Feet
Dedos de los pies	deh-dohs deh lohs pee-ehs	Toes

Mouth components (*componentes de la boca*):

Body part	Pronunciation	English translation
Labios	lah-bee-ohs	Lips
Dientes	dee-ehn-tehs	Teeth
Encías	ehn-see-ahs	Gums
Lengua	lehn-gwah	Tongue
Paladar	pah-lah-dahr	Palate
Amígdalas	ah-meeg-dah-lahs	Tonsils
Úvula	oo-buh-lah	Uvula
Saliva	sah-lee-vah	Saliva

Skeletal system (*sistema esquelético*):

Body part	Pronunciation	English translation
Huesos	weh-sohs	Bones
Cartílago	kar-tee-lah-go	Cartilage
Articulaciones	ahr-tee-koo-lah-syo-nes	Joints
Tejido nervioso	teh-hee-doh ner-vee-oh-so	Nervous tissue
Craneo	krah-neh-oh	Skull
Columna vertebral	koh-loo-mnah vehr-teh-brahl	Spine
Costillas	kohs-tee-yahs	Ribs
Esternón	ehs-tehr-nohn	Sternum

Cardiovascular system (*sistema cardiovascular*):

Body part	Pronunciation	English translation
Corazón	koh-rah-zohn	Heart
Vasos Sanguíneos	bah-sohs sahn-ghee-neh-ohs	Blood Vessels
Arterias	ahr-teh-ree-ahs	Arteries
Venas	veh-nahs	Veins

Respiratory system (*sistema respiratorio*):

Body part	Pronunciation	English translation
Pulmones	pool-moh-nes	Lungs
Tráquea	trah-keh-ah	Trachea
Bronquios	brohn-kee-ohs	Bronchi
Diafragma	dee-ah-frag-mah	Diaphragm

Nervous system (*sistema nervioso*):

Body part	Pronunciation	English translation
Cerebro	seh-reh-broh	Brain
Médula Espinal	meh-doo-lah ehs-pee-nahl	Spinal Cord
Nervios	nehr-bee-ohs	Nerves
Músculos	moo-skoo-lohs	Muscles

Digestive system (*sistema digestivo*):

Body part	Pronunciation	English translation
Estómago	ehs-toh-mah-goh	Stomach
Intestino Delgado	een-tehs-tee-noh dehl-gah-doh	Small Intestine
Intestino Grueso	een-tehs-tee-noh grew-eh-soh	Large Intestine
Hígado	ee-gah-doh	Liver
Vesícula Biliar	veh-see-koo-lah bee-lee-ahr	Gallbladder
Páncreas	pahn-kreh-ahs	Pancreas

Urinary system (*sistema urinario*):

Body part	Pronunciation	English translation
Riñones	ree-nyee-oh-nehs	Kidneys
Vejiga	veh-hee-gah	Bladder
Uretra	oo-reh-trah	Urethra

Body secretions and fluids (*secreciones y fluidos del cuerpo*):

Secretion/Fluid	Pronunciation	English translation
Sangre	sahn-greh	Blood
Saliva	sah-lee-vah	Saliva
Lágrimas	lah-gree-mahs	Tears
Sudor	soo-dohr	Sweat
Orina	oh-ree-nah	Urine
Mucosidad	moo-koh-see-dahd	Mucus
Pus	poos	Pus
Ácido Gástrico	ah-see-doh gah-stree-koh	Gastric Acid

Practice this vocabulary and if it helps you, I recommend that you look for images of the body and label them. This will be of enormous help to you since having graphic support increases your chances of learning and correctly associating words with their meaning. You can choose different label colors for the different systems and parts of the body, making the association clearer and easier for your brain to internalize (Dzulkifli & Mustafar, 2013).

Before continuing, let's put this new vocabulary to use by applying it to the following example:

- **Paciente:** *¡Hola, doctor! Me* **siento mal.** *Tengo* **dolor** *en todo el cuerpo y me siento muy* **cansado.**

(Hello, doctor! I'm not feeling well. I have pain all over my body and I feel very tired)

- **Doctor:** *Hola, ¿desde cuándo siente estos* **síntomas**? *¿Puede describir dónde siente el dolor?*

(Hello, since when have you been experiencing these symptoms? Can you describe where you feel the pain?)

- **P:** *He tenido estos síntomas durante una semana. El dolor está en mis* **articulaciones** *y* **músculos**, *especialmente en las* **piernas** *y los* **brazos**.

(I've had these symptoms for a week. The pain is in my joints and muscles, especially in my legs and arms.)

- **D:** *Entiendo. Vamos a hacer algunas* **pruebas**. *¿Ha tenido* **fiebre** *o* **dolor de garganta**?

(I understand. We'll run some tests. Have you had a fever or a sore throat?)

- **P:** *Sí, he tenido fiebre y dolor de garganta también.*

(Yes, I've had a fever and a sore throat as well.)

- **D:** *Gracias por la información. Vamos a hacer un* **análisis de sangre** *para entender mejor lo que está ocurriendo. También revisaremos su garganta y articulaciones en detalle.*

(Thank you for the information. We'll do some blood tests to better understand what's happening. We'll also examine your throat and joints in detail.)

DECODING MEDICAL PROCEDURES IN SPANISH

The next thing we will address will be the different medical procedures that we can perform on the patient. For reasons of practicality and so that you can consult it when you need it, I have arranged them in alphabetical order and added their translation and correct pronunciation.

Procedure	Spanish translation	Spanish pronunciation
Biopsy	Biopsia	Bee-ohp-see-ah
Blood Test	Análisis de Sangre	Ah-nah-lee-sees deh Sahn-greh
Chemotherapy	Quimioterapia	Kee-mee-oh-teh-rah-pee-ah
Colonoscopy	Colonoscopia	Koh-loh-nohs-koh-pee-ah
Dental Procedure	Procedimiento Dental	Pro-seh-dee-mee-ehn-toh Dehn-tahl
Dialysis	Diálisis	Dee-ah-lee-sees
Endoscopy	Endoscopia	Ehn-dohs-koh-pee-ah
Examination	Examen	Eh-kzah-mehn
Heart Transplant	Trasplante de Corazón	Trahs-plahn-teh deh Koh-rah-sohn
MRI	Resonancia Magnética	Reh-soh-nahn-see-ah mahg-neh-tee-kah
Physical Therapy	Terapia Física	Teh-rah-pee-ah Fee-see-kah
Radiation Therapy	Radioterapia	Rah-dee-oh-teh-rah-pee-ah
Surgery	Cirugía	See-roo-hee-ah
Vaccination	Vacunación	Bah-koo-nah-see-ohn
X-ray	Radiografía	Rah-dee-oh-grah-fee-ah

From the following conversation between a nurse and a mother, you can begin to generate an intuition of how to use these words:

- **Enfermera:** *Hola, soy la enfermera Laura. ¿Usted es la madre de Juan?*

(Hello, I'm Nurse Laura. Are you Juan's mother?)

- **Madre:** *Sí, soy su madre. ¿Cómo está mi hijo?*

(Yes, I'm his mother. How is my son?)

- **E:** *Su hijo está estable en este momento, pero tuvo un* **accidente** *en bicicleta. Tiene algunas* **lesiones** *en el cuerpo y una* **cadera rota**. *Necesitamos hacer una* **radiografía**, *una* **transfusión de sangre** *y una* **resonancia magnética** *en su cabeza antes de la* **cirugía** *para reparar su hueso.*

(Your son is stable at the moment, but he had a bike accident. He has some injuries on his body and a broken hip. We need to do an X-ray, a blood transfusion, and an MRI on his head before the surgery to repair his bone.)

- **M:** *¡Dios mío, eso suena grave! ¿Está sufriendo mucho* **dolor***?*

(Oh my God, that sounds serious! Is he in a lot of pain?)

- **E:** *Estamos controlando su dolor y lo mantendremos cómodo. Estamos haciendo todo lo posible por su* **bienestar**.

(We are managing his pain and we will keep him comfortable. We are doing everything we can for his well-being.)

- **M:** *Gracias por cuidar de mi hijo. ¿Puedo verlo antes de los* ***procedimientos?***

(Thank you for taking care of my son. Can I see him before the procedures?)

- **E:** *Claro, le permitiremos verlo antes de que comencemos con los procedimientos médicos. Estamos aquí para apoyarlos en todo momento.*

(Of course, we will allow you to see him before we start with the medical procedures. We are here to support you both at all times.)

PHARMACOLOGICAL VOCABULARY: SPANISH FOR MEDICATIONS

This section will introduce you to the pharmacological vocabulary you need to give prescriptions and medications effectively to your patients.

While you may not be expected to become a full-fledged pharmacist, having a grasp of medication-related terms will significantly enhance your ability to communicate treatment plans to Spanish-speaking patients. So, let's move on to ensuring that no language barrier stands in the way of delivering the best care possible.

Let's start by addressing some of the most common terms related to medications and prescriptions.

Spanish term	Pronunciation	English translation
Analgésico	ah-nahl-geh-see-koh	Analgesic (painkiller)
Antibiótico	ahn-tee-bee-oh-tee-koh	Antibiotic
Anticoagulante	ahn-tee-koh-ah-goo-lahn-teh	Anticoagulant
Contraindicaciones	kohn-trah-yn-dee-kah-syoh-nehs	Contraindications
Dosificación	doh-see-fee-kah-see-ohn	Dosage
Dosis	doh-sees	Dose
Efectos secundarios	eh-fehk-tohs seh-koon-dah-ree-ohs	Side effects
Farmacia	fahr-mah-see-ah	Pharmacy
Genérico	heh-neh-ree-koh	Generic
Ingredientes	een-greh-dee-ehn-tes	Ingredients
Insulina	een-soo-lee-nah	Insulin
Interacciones	een-ter-ahk-syoh-nehss	Interactions
Medicina	meh-dee-see-nah	Medicine
Pastilla	pahs-tee-yah	Pill
Posología	poh-soh-loh-hee-ah	Dosage instructions
Receta	reh-seh-tah	Prescription
Receta médica	reh-seh-tah meh-dee-kah	Medical prescription
Suspensión	soo-spehn-syohn	Suspension
Jarabe	hah-rah-beh	Syrup

Now let's look at some examples applying those terms:

- *Necesita tomar este **analgésico** para el dolor* (You need to take this painkiller for the pain.)
- *¿Es este un **antibiótico** para mi infección?* (Is this an antibiotic for my infection?)
- *La **insulina** es importante para controlar la diabetes.* (Insulin is important for controlling diabetes.)
- *¿Puedo recoger mi **medicina** en la **farmacia**?* (Can I pick up my medicine at the pharmacy?)
- *Esta es una **receta** para su medicina* (This is a prescription for your medicine.)

EXERCISES AND PRACTICE

A. Read and complete the translation below:

Paciente: Hola, doctor. Me siento mal. Tengo dolor de cabeza y fiebre desde ayer. Además, mis músculos y articulaciones me duelen mucho.

Doctor: Entiendo, siento que te sientas mal. Vamos a ver qué está pasando. ¿Puedes decirme más sobre tu dolor de cabeza? ¿Es un dolor punzante o constante?

P: Es constante, como una presión en la frente. También me duele la garganta y tengo tos.

D: Gracias por la información. Parece que tienes varios síntomas. Vamos a revisarte. Primero, midamos tu temperatura. Luego, haremos algunos exámenes para determinar la causa de tus síntomas.

P: ¿Necesitaré tomar medicamentos?

D: Eso dependerá de lo que encontremos en los exámenes. Lo importante ahora es obtener un diagnóstico preciso. Trabajaré contigo para ayudarte a sentirte mejor. Por favor, espera un momento mientras preparo los exámenes.

Translation

P: Hello, doctor. I don't feel well. I have a _____(1) and fever since yesterday. Also, my muscles and _____ (2) hurt a lot.

D: I understand, I'm sorry you are feeling bad. Let's see what's happening. Can you tell me more about your headache? Is it a stabbing or constant pain?

P: It's constant, like pressure on the forehead. My _____(3) also hurts and I have a cough.

D: Thanks for the information. It sounds like you have several symptoms. Let's check you out. First, let's measure your temperature. Then, we will do some _____(4) to determine the cause of your symptoms.

P: Will I need to take _____(5)?

D: That will depend on what we find in the exams. The important thing now is to obtain an accurate _____(6). I will work with you to help you feel better. Please wait a moment while I prepare for the exams.

Answers:

1. headache
2. joints

3. throat

4. tests

5. medication

6. diagnosis

B. Develop a set of flashcards with medical terms in Spanish on one side and their English translations on the other. Use these flashcards for self-testing and review.

DIALOGUES FOR DIAGNOSIS: SPANISH FOR PATIENT INTERACTION

As we have realized through this exploration, for healthcare professionals, the ability to communicate with patients is crucial in providing the best care possible. However, when language barriers come into play, these interactions can become challenging. This chapter aims to bridge that gap by offering practical Spanish phrases and dialogues specifically tailored for various medical scenarios, empowering healthcare professionals to provide more effective and empathetic care for Spanish-speaking patients.

A nurse friend once regaled me with a story from her own experience. In a situation where a patient required immediate attention for what seemed to be a severe symptom, an interpreter was called to facilitate communication. However, a misunderstanding arose between the patient, the interpreter, and the medical staff regarding the symptom's nature and severity. This incident highlighted the critical need for healthcare professionals to have autonomy in communicating with their patients, without solely relying on interpreters. To avoid those scenarios, I aim to equip you with the skills and confidence to navigate such scenarios smoothly, ensuring that both you and your patients understand each other clearly.

BREAKING THE ICE: INITIAL PATIENT INTERACTION

Initiating a medical conversation with a Spanish-speaking patient is the first step in establishing a rapport and ensuring a positive healthcare experience. This initial contact sets the tone for the entire interaction, making it essential to begin on a strong note.

To create a warm and welcoming atmosphere, start with simple greetings such as "*Buenos días*" (good morning) or "*Hola, ¿cómo puedo ayudarle hoy?*" (Hello, how can I help you today?). These greetings convey respect and set the stage for a productive conversation.

Asking about the patient's overall feeling or well-being is a crucial part of the initial interaction. Use phrases like "*¿Cómo se siente hoy?*" (How are you feeling today?) to assess their current state. Additionally, inquiring about pain levels with "*En una escala del 1 al 10, cuanto dolor siente hoy?*" (On a scale of 1 to 10, how much pain are you feeling today?) is essential to understanding their discomfort accurately.

Encourage open dialogue by posing open-ended questions. For example, "*¿Puede contarme más sobre...?*" (Can you tell me more about...?) invites patients to share additional details about their symptoms or concerns. This approach fosters a sense of collaboration, where patients actively participate in their healthcare.

Also, it's crucial to use words of reassurance to convey empathy and understanding. Phrases like "*Entiendo lo que está pasando*" (I understand what you're going through) can help patients feel seen and heard, reducing anxiety and building trust. Expressing affirmations like "*Estamos aquí para ayudarle*" (We are here to help you) reassures patients that they are in capable and compassionate hands, fostering a positive patient-provider relationship from the outset.

Here you have a practical chart, useful to have on hand, with some useful expressions to break the ice and establish accurate and empathetic contact with the patient:

Spanish expression	Pronunciation	English translation
Buenos días	Bweh-nohs dee-ahs	Good morning
Hola, ¿cómo puedo ayudarle hoy?	Oh-lah, koh-moh pweh-doh ah-yoo-dahr-leh oh-ee	Hello, how can I help you today?
¿Cómo se siente hoy?	Koh-moh seh syehn-teh oh-ee	How are you feeling today?
En una escala del 1 al 10, cuanto dolor siente hoy?	Ehn oo-nah ehs-kah-lah dehl ooh-noh ahl dee-ehz, kwahn-toh doh-lohr syehn-teh oh-ee	On a scale of 1 to 10, how much pain are you feeling today?
¿Puede contarme más sobre...?	Poo-eh-deh kohn-tahr-meh mahs soh-breh...?	Can you tell me more about...?
Entiendo lo que está pasando	Ehn-tee-ehn-doh loh keh eh-stah pah-sahn-doh	I understand what you're going through
Estamos aquí para ayudarle	Ehs-tah-mohs ah-kee pah-rah ah-yoo-dahr-leh	We are here to help you

SPEAKING OF SYMPTOMS: DISCUSSING MEDICAL HISTORY AND CURRENT SYMPTOMS

As you know, understanding a patient's medical history and current symptoms is essential for an accurate diagnosis and effective treatment. When communicating with Spanish-speaking patients, it's crucial to ask the right questions and actively listen to their responses.

To start the discussion about a patient's medical history, it's essential to use polite and open-ended questions to gather relevant information. Here are some phrases to use:

- *¿Puede contarme sobre su historial médico?* (Can you tell me about your medical history?)
- *¿Ha tenido problemas médicos en el pasado?* (Have you had medical problems in the past?)
- *¿Alguna vez ha sido hospitalizado?* (Have you ever been hospitalized?)

When discussing the patient's current symptoms, it's important to ask specific and direct questions to pinpoint their condition accurately. Here are some helpful phrases for this part of the conversation:

- *¿Cuándo empezaron los síntomas?* (When did the symptoms start?)
- *¿Dónde siente dolor?* (Where do you feel pain?)
- *¿Cómo describiría la intensidad del dolor?* (How would you describe the intensity of the pain?)

Active listening is a vital skill when discussing medical history and symptoms with patients. After the patient provides their responses, it's essential to confirm your understanding to ensure clarity and accuracy. Use phrases like:

- *Si entiendo correctamente, usted está experimentando...* (If I understand correctly, you are experiencing...)
- *Entendido. Entonces, haremos lo siguiente...* (Understood. So, we'll do the following...)

To complete the patient's medical profile, it's important to ask about any medications they are currently taking. Here are relevant phrases:

- *¿Está tomando algún medicamento actualmente?* (Are you currently taking any medication?)
- *¿Cuántas veces al día toma este medicamento?* (How many times a day do you take this medication?)

Let's continue building the wall of knowledge of this wonderful language. In previous sections, we armed ourselves with the learning of basic words to understand which part of the patient's body is affected and what treatments we can conduct on them. Now, we will examine what potential symptoms the patient may show. Below are the most common symptoms:

Spanish symptom	Pronunciation	English translation
Dolor abdominal	doh-lohr ahb-doh-mee-nahl	Abdominal pain
Hemorragia/sangrado	eh-moh-rah-hee-ah/sahn-grah-doh	Bleeding
Dolor en el pecho	doh-lohr ehn ehl peh-choh	Chest pain
Escalofríos	ehs-kah-loh-free-ohs	Chills
Estreñimiento	eh-streh-nyee-mee-ehn-toh	Constipation
Dificultad para respirar	dee-fee-kool-tahd pah-rah rehs-pee-rahr	Difficulty breathing
Mareos	mah-reh-ohs	Dizziness
Sudoración excesiva	soo-doh-rah-see-ohn ehk-seh-see-vah	Excessive sweating
Sangrado de encías	sahn-grah-doh deh ehn-see-ahs	Gum bleeding
Ronquera	ron-keh-rah	Hoarseness
Inflamación	een-flah-mah-see-on	Swelling
Irritación	ee-ree-tah-see-ohn	Irritation
Secreción nasal	seh-kreh-see-ohn nah-sahl	Nasal discharge
Picazón en la piel	pee-kah-sohn ehn lah pee-ehl	Skin itching
Vértigo	vehr-tee-goh	Vertigo

Here's a chart with common **types of pain** in Spanish, their pronunciation, and English translations:

Spanish term	Pronunciation	English translation
Agudo	ah-goo-doh	Acute/sharp
Crónico	kroh-nee-koh	Chronic
Punzante	poon-sahn-teh	Piercing, stabbing
Intenso	een-ten-soh	Intense
Leve	leh-veh	Mild
Persistente	pehr-sis-ten-teh	Persistent
Intermitente	een-ter-mee-ten-teh	Intermittent
Opresivo	oh-preh-see-voh	Oppressive, crushing
Agobiante	ah-goh-bee-ahn-teh	Overwhelming
Lancinante	lahn-see-nahn-teh	Lancinating
Ardiente	ahr-dee-ehn-teh	Burning
Molesto	moh-lehs-toh	Annoying
Penetrante	peh-neh-trahn-teh	Penetrating
Incómodo	een-koh-moh-doh	Uncomfortable

Below, you can check some examples of potential real scenarios where patients describe their current symptoms:

- **Patient:** *Buenos días, doctor. Desde ayer he estado sintiendo un dolor agudo en el pecho y dificultad para respirar. También tengo sudores fríos. No sé qué está pasando.*

Translation: Good morning, doctor. Since yesterday, I've been feeling sharp chest pain and difficulty breathing. I also have cold sweats. I don't know what's happening.

- *Patient: Hola, enfermera. Tengo fiebre alta desde hace tres días, me duele la garganta y tengo congestión nasal. Además, tengo dolor en todo el cuerpo.*

Translation: Hi, nurse. I've had a high fever for three days, my throat hurts, and I have a stuffy nose. Also, my whole body aches.

- *Patient: Doctor, desde la semana pasada he notado que tengo sangre en las heces y me siento cansado todo el tiempo. Además, he perdido peso sin razón aparente.*

Translation: Doctor, since last week, I've noticed blood in my stool and I feel tired all the time. Also, I've lost weight for no apparent reason.

- *Patient: Buenas tardes. Me desmayé en el trabajo hoy, y me duele mucho la cabeza desde hace varios días. Además, tengo visión borrosa y mareos frecuentes.*

Translation: Good afternoon. I fainted at work today and I've had a severe headache for several days. Also, I have blurry vision and frequent dizziness.

- **Patient**: *Enfermera, estoy experimentando un fuerte dolor abdominal en el lado derecho, y siento náuseas constantes. También tengo fiebre y escalofríos.*

Translation: Nurse, I'm experiencing severe abdominal pain on the right side and I have constant nausea. I also have a fever and chills.

READING THE RESULTS: EXPLAINING DIAGNOSES AND TREATMENT PLANS

Clear communication is crucial when explaining diagnoses and treatment plans to patients, especially when language barriers may exist. Effective communication ensures that patients fully understand their medical condition and the proposed course of treatment. Healthcare professionals can use specific phrases and techniques to facilitate this process.

When discussing diagnoses, it's essential to be direct and clear. Start by using phrases like *"Los resultados muestran que usted tiene..."* (The results show that you have...). This provides patients with a straightforward introduction to their diagnosis, avoiding any ambiguity.

Explaining treatment plans should also involve simple, easy-to-understand language. Use phrases such as *"El plan de tratamiento incluirá..."* (The treatment plan will include...) or *"Es importante que usted..."* (It is important that you...) to outline the proposed course of action. Avoid medical jargon and technical terms unless the patient is familiar with them.

Always check for understanding and encourage questions from the patient. After explaining the diagnosis and treatment plan, ask, "*¿Entiende lo que acabo de explicar?*" (Do you understand what I just explained?). This step is crucial to ensure that the patient comprehends the information provided. If there is any uncertainty or confusion, it can be addressed promptly.

Furthermore, it's essential to actively encourage patients to ask questions or express any concerns they may have. Use phrases like "*¿Tiene alguna pregunta o preocupación?*" (Do you have any questions or concerns?). This not only invites patients to seek clarification but also demonstrates your commitment to their well-being and comfort.

Here's a chart with key expressions for explaining diagnoses and treatment plans to patients in Spanish, along with their pronunciation and English translations:

Spanish expression	Pronunciation	English translation
Los resultados muestran que usted tiene...	lohs reh-sool-tah-dohs moo-ehs-trahn keh oos-tehd tyeh-neh...	The results show that you have...
El plan de tratamiento incluirá...	ehl plahn deh trah-tah-mee-ehn-toh een-kloo-ee-rah...	The treatment plan will include...
Es importante que usted...	ehs eem-pohr-tahn-teh keh oos-tehd...	It is important that you...
¿Entiende lo que acabo de explicar?	ehn-tee-ehn-deh loh keh ah-kah-boh deh ehks-plee-kahr...	Do you understand what I just explained?
¿Tiene alguna pregunta o preocupación?	tee-eh-neh al-goo-nah preh-goon-tah o preh-oh-koo-pah-see-ohn	Do you have any questions or concerns?

Le explicaré su diagnóstico más detalladamente.	leh ehks-plee-kah-reh soo dyahg-nohs-tee-koh mahs deh-tah-yah-dah-mehn-teh	I will explain your diagnosis in more detail.
El tratamiento tiene como objetivo...	el trah-tah-mee-ehn-toh tee-eh-neh koh-moh oh-bheh-tee-voh	The treatment aims to...
Para su bienestar, es fundamental seguir tratamiento.	pah-rah soo bee-ehn-ehs-tahr, ehs foon-dah-mehn-tahl seh-gheer el trah-tah-mee-ehn-toh	For your well-being, it is essential to follow the treatment.
¿Hay algo que no comprende o le preocupa?	ay ahl-goh keh noh kohm-prehn-deh o leh preh-oh-koo-pah	Is there anything you don't understand or are concerned about?

In the following chart, you can find some of the most common diagnoses ordered alphabetically. This chart can be really handy when explaining your patients their clinical situation:

Diagnosis	Spanish translation	Spanish pronunciation
Allergy	Alergia	ah-lehr-hee-ah
Arthritis	Artritis	ahr-tree-tees
Asthma	Asma	ahs-mah
Bronchitis	Bronquitis	brohn-kee-teess
Cancer	Cáncer	kahn-sehr
Diabetes	Diabetes	dee-ah-beh-tehs
Epilepsy	Epilepsia	eh-pee-lep-see-ah
Fracture	Fractura	frahk-too-rah
Gastritis	Gastritis	gahs-tree-tees
Hypertension	Hipertensión	ee-pehr-tehn-see-ohn
Infection	Infección	een-fehk-see-ohn
Migraine	Migraña	mee-grah-nyah
Pneumonia	Neumonía	neh-oo-moh-nee-ah
Pregnancy	Embarazo	ehm-bah-rah-so
Rheumatism	Reumatismo	reh-oo-mah-tees-moh
Stroke	Accidente cerebrovascular (ACV)	ahk-see-den-teh seh-reh-broh-vahs-koo-lahr (ah seh beh)
Ulcer	Úlcera	ool-seh-rah
Anemia	Anemia	ah-neh-mee-ah
Hypothyroidism	Hipotiroidismo	ee-poh-tee-roy-dees-moh
Osteoporosis	Osteoporosis	ohs-teh-oh-poh-roh-sees

In the following chart, you'll find treatments and medical procedures along with their proper pronunciation and translation:

Treatment/Procedure	Spanish translation	Spanish pronunciation
Chemotherapy	Quimioterapia	kee-mee-oh-teh-rah-pee-ah
Dental extraction	Extracción dental	ehks-trahk-syon dehn-tahl
Dialysis	Diálisis	dee-ah-lee-sees
Electrocardiogram (ECG or EKG)	Electrocardiograma	eh-lehk-troh-kahr-dee-oh-grah-mah
Endoscopy	Endoscopia	ehn-dohs-koh-pee-ah
Hernia repair	Reparación de hernia	reh-pah-rah-see-ohn deh ehr-nyah
Joint replacement	Reemplazo de articulación	reh-ehm-plah-soh deh ahr-tee-koo-lah-syon
Laser surgery	Cirugía láser	see-roo-hee-ah lah-sehr
Mammogram	Mamografía	mah-moh-grah-fee-ah
Organ transplant	Trasplante de órganos	trahs-plan-teh deh ohr-gah-nohs
Physical examination	Examen físico	ehk-sah-mehn fee-see-koh
Physical therapy	Terapia física	teh-rah-pee-ah fee-see-kah
Respiratory therapy	Terapia respiratoria	teh-rah-pee-ah reh-spee-rah-toh-ree-ah
Vaccination	Vacunación	vah-koo-nah-see-ohn

Keep in mind that in the previous chapter, we already addressed some of the most common treatments and medical procedures, so you can check those charts to complete the vocabulary.

The following dialogs will provide you with examples of use for these new words:

Scenario 1:

Doctor: Buenas tardes, señor García. Los resultados muestran que usted tiene diabetes tipo 2. (Good afternoon, Mr. García. The results show that you have type 2 diabetes.)

Paciente: ¿Diabetes? ¿Qué significa eso? (Diabetes? What does that mean?)

D: Significa que su cuerpo tiene dificultades para controlar el azúcar en la sangre. Pero no se preocupe, podemos tratarla. (It means that your body has trouble controlling blood sugar. But don't worry, we can treat it.)

Scenario 2:

Enfermero: Hola, señora López. Quiero informarle que después de las pruebas, hemos confirmado que tiene hipertensión. (Hello, Mrs. López. I want to inform you that after the tests, we have confirmed that you have hypertension.)

Paciente: Entendido, ¿qué debo hacer ahora? (Understood, what should I do now?)

E: Necesitará cambios en su dieta y medicamentos para controlarla. Estamos aquí para ayudarle en cada paso del camino. (You'll need changes in your diet and medications to control it. We are here to help you every step of the way.)

Scenario 3:

Doctor: *Buen día, señor Rodríguez. Los análisis muestran que tiene una infección en el tracto urinario.* (Good morning, Mr. Rodríguez. The tests show that you have a urinary tract infection.)

Le recetaré antibióticos para tratarla, y es importante que tome todos los medicamentos según las indicaciones. (I will prescribe antibiotics to treat it, and it's important that you take all the medications as directed.)

Scenario 4

Enfermera: *Señorita Pérez. Los exámenes de sangre revelan que tiene anemia.* (Miss Pérez. Blood tests reveal that you have anemia.)

Paciente: Anemia, *¿qué implica eso?* (Anemia, what does that entail?)

E: Significa que sus glóbulos rojos están bajos, lo que puede causar fatiga. Le daremos suplementos de hierro y pautas dietéticas para mejorar su salud. (It means that your red blood cell count is low, which can lead to fatigue. We will provide iron supplements and dietary guidelines to improve your health.)

UNDER PRESSURE: HANDLING EMERGENCIES AND CRITICAL SITUATIONS

Imagine a scenario in which a patient suddenly experiences severe chest pain. You, as a healthcare professional, spring into action. In such situations, there's no time for lengthy explanations. Instead, you need to use short, clear instructions. Phrases like "*Necesito que se calme y respire profundamente*" (I need you to calm down and breathe deeply) can help the patient focus and alleviate their anxiety. By communicating the urgency of the situation, you prepare the patient for the actions you're about to take. For instance, "*Vamos a llevarle a la sala de urgencias ahora*" (We are going to take you to the emergency room now) conveys a sense of immediacy and the need for swift action.

As your experiences have shown you, emergencies can be frightening for patients and their families. Providing reassurance is a crucial aspect of communication. In the midst of chaos, conveying empathy and care can make all the difference. Phrases like "*Estamos haciendo todo lo posible para ayudarle*" (We are doing everything we can to help you) reassure the patient that they are in capable hands. It helps them understand that their well-being is the top priority.

During emergencies, it's not just the patient who needs information; their family often seeks updates as well. Effective communication means keeping both the patient and their loved ones informed. For example, when the doctor is on the way, you can say, "*El médico estará aquí pronto*" (The doctor will be here soon). This lets the patient and their family know that help is on the way and provides them with a sense of relief.

Furthermore, when medical tests and procedures are being conducted, patients and their families may be anxious and uncertain about the situation. By saying, "*Estamos haciendo pruebas para entender mejor lo que está pasando*" (We are doing tests to better understand what is going on), you offer transparency and a glimpse into the medical process. It empowers the patient and their family with knowledge, reducing anxiety and enhancing trust in the healthcare team.

In critical situations, every word you say matters. It can comfort, reassure, and provide clarity. Effective communication is not just about relaying information; it's about maintaining trust and compassion, even in the most challenging of circumstances.

Here's a chart including the expressions for handling emergencies and critical situations in Spanish, along with their English translations and pronunciations:

Spanish phrase	English translation	Spanish pronunciation
Necesito que se calme y respire profundamente	I need you to calm down and breathe deeply	neh-seh-see-toh keh seh kahl-meh ee rehs-pee-reh proh-foon-dah-mehn-teh
Vamos a llevarle a la sala de urgencias ahora	We are going to take you to the emergency room now	vah-mohs ah yeh-vahr-leh ah lah sah-lah deh oor-hehn-see-ahs ah-oh-rah
Estamos haciendo todo lo posible para ayudarle	We are doing everything we can to help you	ehs-tah-mohs ah-see-ehn-doh toh-doh loh poh-see-bleh pah-rah ah-yoo-dahr-leh
El médico estará aquí pronto	The doctor will be here soon	ehl meh-dee-koh ehs-tah-rah ah-kee prohn-toh
Estamos haciendo pruebas para entender mejor lo que está pasando	We are doing tests to better understand what is going on	ehs-tah-mohs ah-see-ehn-doh prweh-bahs pah-rah ehn-tehn-dehr meh-hor loh keh ehs-tah pah-sahn-doh

EXERCISES AND PRACTICE

A. Read the following dialogue and then complete the translation in Spanish with the missing words:

Healthcare Professional (HP): Good morning. How can I assist you today?

Patient (P): Good morning. I'm here because I don't feel very well.

HP: I understand. What are your symptoms?

P: I have a headache, a fever, and chest pain.

HP: I'm sorry to hear that. Let's figure out what's going on. When did these symptoms start?

P: They began yesterday afternoon. I got worried because the chest pain is new for me.

HP: Thank you for sharing that. Have you had similar health issues in the past?

P: No, I've never had this before. I'm a little scared.

HP: I understand why you would be concerned. We're here to help you. We're going to run some tests to better understand what's happening. Is there anything else you'd like to tell me about your symptoms?

P: No, that's all for now.

HP: Very well. We'll take care of you and determine the cause of your symptoms. If you have any questions or concerns at any time, please don't hesitate to let us know.

Translation:

HP: Buenos días. ¿Cómo puedo ayudarle hoy?

P: Buenos días. Estoy aquí porque no me siento muy bien.

HP: Entiendo. ¿Cuáles son sus _____(1)?

P: Me _____(2) y tengo _____(3). Además, tengo dolor en el _____(4).

HP: Siento escuchar eso. Vamos a averiguar lo que está pasando. ¿Desde cuándo empezaron estos síntomas?

P: Empezaron ayer por la tarde. Me preocupé porque el dolor en el pecho es nuevo para mí.

HP: Gracias por compartir eso. ¿Ha tenido _____(5) similares en el pasado?

P: No, nunca había tenido esto antes. Estoy un poco asustado.

HP: Entiendo por qué estaría preocupado. _____(6). Vamos a hacer algunas _____(7) para comprender mejor lo que está sucediendo. ¿Alguna otra cosa que quiera contarme sobre sus síntomas?

P: No, eso es todo por ahora.

HP: Muy bien. Vamos a cuidar de usted y averiguar la causa de sus síntomas. Si tiene alguna pregunta o preocupación en cualquier momento, no dude en decírnoslo.

Answers:

1. *síntomas*
2. *duele la cabeza*
3. *fiebre*
4. *pecho*
5. *problemas de salud*
6. *Estamos aquí para ayudarle*
7. *pruebas*

B. Read the following dialogue between a doctor and a worried family about the situation of a loved one. Try to read out loud and, if possible, ask a native speaker to record it for you so you get familiar with the pronunciation and accent. The English translation is available below, and you can check it to reinforce the learned vocabulary:

HP: Buenos días, familia. Soy la doctora Green, y estamos atendiendo a su ser querido en este momento. Entiendo que están preocupados, pero permítanme brindarles información importante.

Family: ¿Cómo está? ¿Qué está pasando?

HP: Entendemos que esto es angustiante. Su familiar está siendo atendida por nuestro equipo médico. Estamos realizando pruebas para determinar la causa de su malestar. Por favor, siéntanse tranquilos sabiendo que estamos haciendo todo lo posible para ayudarle.

F: ¿Puede decirnos qué está sucediendo?

HP: Claro. Su ser querido ha experimentado un dolor en el pecho y dificultad para respirar. Estos síntomas son preocupantes, y estamos evaluándolos cuidadosamente. Hemos hecho un electrocardiograma y otros estudios para obtener una imagen completa de su situación.

F: ¿Qué tipo de tratamiento va a recibir?

HP: Eso dependerá del diagnóstico final. Una vez que tengamos todos los resultados, discutiremos el plan de tratamiento con ustedes. Queremos asegurarnos de que reciba la atención adecuada y el mejor cuidado posible.

F: Gracias por su atención. Estamos asustados, pero confiamos en ustedes.

HP: Entendemos completamente sus preocupaciones. Estamos aquí para apoyarles y mantenerles informados en todo momento. Por favor, siéntanse libres de hacer cualquier pregunta o expresar cualquier inquietud que tengan. Estamos comprometidos en brindar el mejor cuidado a su ser querido.

Translation:

HP: Good morning, family. I'm Dr. Green, and we're caring for your loved one right now. I understand that you are worried but let me provide you with some important information.

F: How is she? What's going on?

HP: We understand that this is distressing. Your family member is being cared for by our medical team. We are conducting tests to determine the cause of her discomfort. Please rest assured knowing that we are doing everything we can to help her.

F: Can you tell us what is happening?

HP: Sure. Your loved one has experienced chest pain and difficulty breathing. These symptoms are concerning and we are carefully evaluating them. We have done an EKG and other tests to get a complete picture of her situation.

F: What type of treatment is she going to receive?

HP: That will depend on the final diagnosis. Once we have all the results, we will discuss the treatment plan with you. We want to make sure she receives the proper attention and the best care possible.

F: Thank you for your attention. We are scared, but we trust you.

HP: We completely understand your concerns. We are here to support you and keep you informed at all times. Please feel free to ask any questions or express any concerns you may have. We are committed to providing the best care for your loved one.

4

SPECIALIZED TERMS, TAILORED DIALOGUES

I n healthcare, communication isn't merely about language; it's about understanding and addressing the specific needs of patients in various medical contexts. Whether you're in cardiology, pediatrics, obstetrics, or any other specialized field, effective communication is the linchpin of quality care. This chapter serves as a valuable resource to help bridge language barriers and ensure the best possible outcomes for your patients.

From discussing pediatric care to explaining surgical procedures in cardiology, we will explore specialized terms and dialogues relevant to different medical fields. By the end of this chapter, you will have a comprehensive toolkit to engage with patients across a spectrum of healthcare scenarios, fostering trust, empathy, and effective communication.

Let's embark on this journey to enhance your language skills and elevate your ability to provide exceptional care in specialized areas of healthcare.

PEDIATRICS: SPEAKING SPANISH FOR THE LITTLE ONES

In this section, we delve into the nuances of pediatric care, focusing on the specialized vocabulary and empathetic dialogues that healthcare professionals should employ when dealing with young patients and their anxious parents.

One fundamental aspect of pediatric care is understanding and using specialized medical terminology effectively. For example, when discussing common childhood illnesses such as measles, you'll need to know how it translates to Spanish: "*sarampión*." This ensures that there is no room for misunderstanding, allowing for precise communication.

Parents play a crucial role in a child's healthcare journey, and effective communication with them is paramount. Employing phrases like "*Su hijo se recuperará pronto*" (Your child will recover soon) can offer comfort, hope, and a sense of assurance. These words are not only informative but also provide emotional support during challenging times.

Children can also often feel anxious or scared in a medical setting, making it essential to employ words and phrases that provide comfort and encouragement. For instance, addressing their fear of pain is vital. Utilize phrases like "*No te preocupes, esto no dolerá*" (Don't worry, this won't hurt) to alleviate their concerns when facing medical procedures.

Using positive reinforcement can significantly impact a child's experience. Simple words like "*valiente*" (brave) not only acknowledge their courage but also empower them to face medical procedures with confidence.

In the following chart, you can find some useful phrases and words to use with young patients and their parents:

Phrase	Spanish translation	Pronunciation
How are you feeling today?	*¿Cómo te sientes hoy?*	Koh-moh teh see-ehn-tehs oh-ee
You will recover soon.	*Te recuperarás pronto.*	Teh reh-koo-peh-rah-rahs prohn-toh
Don't worry, it won't hurt.	*No te preocupes, no dolerá.*	Noh teh preh-oh-koo-pehs, noh doh-leh-rah
You are very brave.	*Eres muy valiente.*	Eh-rehs moo-ee vah-lee-en-teh
We're here to help you.	*Estamos aquí para ayudarte.*	Ehs-tah-mohs ah-kee pah-rah ah-yoo-dahr-teh
It's just a small pinch.	*Es solo un pequeño piquete.*	Ehs soh-loh oon peh-keh-nyoh pee-keh-teh
This won't take long.	*Esto no tomará mucho tiempo.*	Ehs-toh noh toh-mah-rah moo-choh tee-ehm-poh
Your parents are waiting.	*Tus padres están esperando.*	Toos pah-dres ehs-tahn ehs-peh-rahn-doh
You're doing great.	*Lo estás haciendo muy bien.*	Loh ehs-tahs ah-see-ehn-doh moo-ee bee-ehn
It's okay to be scared.	*Está bien tener miedo.*	Ehs-tah bee-ehn teh-nehr mee-eh-doh

The following chart contains specific language for pediatric use:

Spanish phrase	Pronunciation	English translation
Resfriado	rehs-free-ah-doh	Cold
Fiebre	fee-eh-breh	Fever
Vacuna	bah-koo-nah	Vaccine
Varicela	vah-ree-seh-lah	Chickenpox
Asma	ahs-mah	Asthma
Dolor de garganta	doh-lohr deh gahr-GAHN-tah	Sore throat
Tos	tohs	Cough
Conjuntivitis	kohn-hoon-tee-vee-teess	Conjunctivitis (Pink eye)
Alergia	ah-lehr-hee-ah	Allergy
Fractura	frahk-too-rah	Fracture
Cirugía	see-roo-hee-ah	Surgery
Radiografía	rah-dee-oh-grah-fee-ah	X-ray
Anestesia	ah-neh-steh-see-ah	Anesthesia
Examen físico	eh-ksah-men fee-see-koh	Physical examination
Hospitalización	oh-spee-tahl-lee-sah-see-ohn	Hospitalization
Terapia física	teh-rah-pee-ah fee-see-kah	Physical therapy
Medicamento	meh-dee-kah-men-toh	Medication
Inmunización	een-moo-nee-sah-syon	Immunization
Tratamiento	trah-tah-myehn-toh	Treatment

As a footnote, I want to highlight the fact that as you can see, dear reader, some words have been repeated along the charts, like "fever" or "pain". This is due to practical reasons; I want you to use this book as a handy guide to check while you talk with your patients in different contexts.

CARDIOLOGY: DECODING THE HEART IN SPANISH

Understanding specialized medical terminology and communicating effectively with patients in the field of cardiology is crucial for accurate diagnosis and treatment. While terms like "*infarto de miocardio*" (myocardial infarction) and "*arritmia*" (arrhythmia) are specific to this field, it's essential to use simple language when discussing complex conditions with Spanish-speaking patients. For instance, using phrases like "*problema del corazón*" (heart problem) can help patients comprehend their condition more quickly.

Moreover, explaining procedures in Spanish can enhance patient comfort and cooperation. Phrases such as "*Vamos a hacer un electrocardiograma*" (We are going to do an EKG) can prepare patients for upcoming tests or examinations, ensuring they are at ease throughout their medical experience.

So, from the following chart, you can learn specific vocabulary associated with this field of medical care, beginning with the most common diseases and cardiovascular affections, ordered alphabetically for practical purposes:

English term	Spanish translation	Pronunciation
Angina	Angina	ahn-hee-nah
Aortic Aneurysm	Aneurisma aórtico	ah-neh-oo-reez-mah ah-ohr-tee-koh
Arrhythmia	Arritmia	ah-reet-mee-ah
Atherosclerosis	Aterosclerosis	ah-teh-rohs-kleh-roh-sis
Cardiac Arrest	Paro cardíaco	pah-roh kahr-dee-ah-koh
Chest Pain	Dolor en el pecho	doh-lohr en el peh-choh
Congenital Heart Defect	Defecto cardíaco congénito	deh-fehk-toh kahr-dee-ah-koh kohn-heh-nee-toh
Coronary Artery Disease	Enfermedad de las arterias coronarias	ehn-fehr-meh-dah deh lahs ahr-teh-ree-ahs koh-roh-nah-ree-ahs
Heart Attack	Ataque al corazón	ah-tah-keh ahl koh-rah-sohn
Heart Disease	Enfermedad cardíaca	ehn-fehr-meh-dah kahr-dee-ah-kah
High Blood Pressure	Presión arterial alta	preh-see-ohn ahr-teh-ree-ahl ahl-tah
Myocardial Infarction	Infarto de miocardio	een-fahr-toh deh mee-oh-kahr-dee-oh
Palpitations	Palpitaciones	pahl-pee-tah-see-oh-nehs
Stroke	Derrame cerebral	deh-rah-meh seh-reh-brahl
Valve Disease	Enfermedad de la válvula	ehn-fehr-meh-dah deh lah vahl-voo-lah

In the following one, you'll find the most common medical procedures, sorted by the same criteria:

English term	Spanish translation	Pronunciation
Angioplasty	Angioplastia	an-hee-oh-plahs-tee-ah
Cardiac Catheterization	Cateterismo Cardíaco	kah-teh-teh-reez-moh kahr-dee-ah-koh
Coronary Artery Bypass Surgery	Cirugía de Bypass de Arterias Coronarias	see-roo-hee-ah deh bye-pass deh ar-teh-ree-ahs koh-roh-nah-ree-ahs
Defibrillation	Desfibrilación	des-fee-bree-lah-syon
Echocardiogram	Ecocardiograma	eh-koh-kahr-dee-oh-gram-ah
Heart Transplant	Trasplante de Corazón	trahs-plan-teh deh koh-rah-sohn
Pacemaker	Marcapasos	mahr-kah-pah-sohs
Stent	Stent	stent
Treadmill Stress Test	Prueba de Esfuerzo en Cinta	prwoo-eh-bah deh ehs-fwehr-soh ehn seen-tah
Valve Replacement Surgery	Cirugía de Reemplazo de Válvula	see-roo-hee-ah deh reh-em-plah-soh deh vahl-voo-lah

NEUROLOGY: NAVIGATING THE BRAIN IN SPANISH

Now it's time to address the proper technical language to communicate with Spanish speakers about their neurological health. Below, you will find some of the most common terms for health issues and treatments:

English term	Spanish translation	Pronunciation
Alzheimer's Disease	*Enfermedad de Alzheimer*	en-fehr-meh-dah deh ahlz-hai-mer
Brain Tumor	*Tumor Cerebral*	too-mohr seh-reh-brahl
Epilepsy	*Epilepsia*	eh-pee-lep-see-ah
Migraine	*Migraña*	mee-grah-nyah
Parkinson's Disease	*Enfermedad de Parkinson*	en-fehr-meh-dah deh pahr-khin-sawn
Seizure	*Convulsión*	kohn-vool-see-own
Synapse	*Sinapsis*	see-nahp-sees
Nervous System	*Sistema Nervioso*	see-steh-mah nehr-vee-oh-soh
Memory Loss	*Pérdida de Memoria*	pehr-dee-dah deh meh-moh-ree-ah
Brain Surgery	*Cirugía Cerebral*	see-roo-hee-ah seh-reh-brahl
EEG (Electroencephalogram)	*EEG (Electroencefalograma)*	ee-ee-gee (eh-lehk-troh-ehn-seh-fah-loh-grah-mah)
Neurological Examination	*Examen Neurológico*	ehk-sah-men nehw-roh-loh-hee-koh
Lumbar Puncture	*Punción Lumbar*	poon-see-ohn loom-bahr
MRI (Magnetic Resonance Imaging)	*Resonancia Magnética*	reh-soh-nahn-see-ah mahg-neh-tee-kah

Brain Scan	Tomografía Cerebral	toh-moh-grah-fee-ah seh-reh-brahl
Physical Therapy	Terapia Física	teh-rah-pee-ah fee-see-kah
Nerve Block	Bloqueo Nervioso	bloh-keh-oh nehr-vee-oh-soh
Deep Brain Stimulation	Estimulación Profunda Cerebral	eh-stee-moo-lah-syon proh-foon-dah seh-reh-brahl
Neurotransmitter Replacement	Reemplazo de Neurotransmisores	reh-ehm-plah-soh deh neh-oo-roh-trahns-mee-soh-rehs

ONCOLOGY: EXPLAINING CANCER CARE IN SPANISH

In the field of oncology, sensitivity in language is of paramount importance due to the delicate nature of cancer care. Patients facing cancer need not only medical explanations but also emotional support.

This medical field comprises a wide array of specific terminologies, ranging from types of cancer to various treatment options. Common terms in this field include "*quimioterapia*" (chemotherapy) and "*radioterapia*" (radiation therapy). When explaining these terms in Spanish, it's crucial to do so with sensitivity and care. Instead of using complex medical jargon, it's often more comforting to describe treatments as "*tratamiento para combatir el cáncer*" (treatment to fight cancer), emphasizing the goal of the intervention.

Beyond the medical aspects, supporting a cancer patient in Spanish involves providing emotional support and reassurance. Phrases like "*Estamos contigo en cada paso del camino*" (We are with you every step of the way) can convey a sense of companionship and comfort during what can be a challenging journey.

Let's address the necessary vocabulary to communicate with patients:

Cancer diseases and conditions

English term	Spanish translation	Pronunciation
Lung Cancer	*Cáncer de Pulmón*	kahn-sehr deh pool-mohn
Breast Cancer	*Cáncer de Mama*	kahn-sehr deh mah-mah
Prostate Cancer	*Cáncer de Próstata*	kahn-sehr deh proh-stah-tah
Leukemia	*Leucemia*	leh-oo-seh-mee-ah
Lymphoma	*Linfoma*	leen-foh-mah
Skin Cancer	*Cáncer de Piel*	kahn-sehr deh pee-ehl
Brain Tumor	*Tumor Cerebral*	too-mohr seh-reh-brahl
Colon Cancer	*Cáncer de Colon*	kahn-sehr deh koh-lon
Ovarian Cancer	*Cáncer de Ovario*	kahn-sehr deh oh-vah-ree-oh
Pancreatic Cancer	*Cáncer de Páncreas*	kahn-sehr deh pahn-kree-ahs
Bladder Cancer	*Cáncer de Vejiga*	kahn-sehr deh veh-hee-gah
Cervical Cancer	*Cáncer Cervical*	kahn-sehr sehr-vee-kahl
Testicular Cancer	*Cáncer Testicular*	kahn-sehr tes-tee-koo-lahr
Thyroid Cancer	*Cáncer de Tiroides*	kahn-sehr deh tee-roy-dehs
Bone Cancer	*Cáncer de Huesos*	kahn-sehr deh weh-sohs

Medical procedures and treatments:

English term	Spanish translation	Pronunciation
Chemotherapy	Quimioterapia	kee-mee-oh-teh-rah-pee-ah
Radiation Therapy	Radioterapia	rah-dee-oh-teh-rah-pee-ah
Surgery	Cirugía	see-roo-hee-ah
Biopsy	Biopsia	bee-op-see-ah
Immunotherapy	Inmunoterapia	een-moo-noh-teh-rah-pee-ah
Targeted Therapy	Terapia Dirigida	teh-rah-pee-ah dee-ree-hee-dah
Stem Cell Transplant	Trasplante de Células Madre	trahs-plan-teh deh seh-loo-lahs mah-dreh
Hormone Therapy	Terapia Hormonal	teh-rah-pee-ah hohr-moh-nahl
Palliative Care	Cuidados Paliativos	kwee-dah-dohs pah-lee-ah-tee-vohs
Genetic Testing	Pruebas Genéticas	prooeh-bahs heh-neh-tee-kahs
Radiosurgery	Radiocirugía	rah-dee-oh-see-roo-hee-ah
Bone Marrow Transplant	Trasplante de Médula Ósea	trahs-plan-teh deh meh-doo-lah oh-seh-ah
Ultrasound	Ecografía	eh-koh-grah-fee-ah
Blood Transfusion	Transfusión de Sangre	trahns-foo-see-ohn deh sahn-greh

Clinical Trials	Ensayos Clínicos	ehn-sah-yohs klee-nee-kohs
Radiation Oncology	Oncología Radioterápica	on-koh-loh-hee-ah rah-dee-oh-teh-rah-pee-kah
Mammogram	Mamografía	mah-moh-grah-fee-ah
Chemoradiation	Quimiorradiación	kee-mee-oh-rah-dee-ah-see-ohn
Supportive Care	Cuidados de Soporte	kwee-dah-dohs deh soh-pohr-teh

EXERCISES AND PRACTICE

A. Read the following story and answer the questions:

Había una vez una enfermera llamada Marta que trabajaba en un hospital pediátrico. Un día, le asignaron la tarea de cuidar a Sofía, una niña de cinco años que había sido diagnosticada con varicela y también tenía un resfriado común. Sofía estaba muy asustada porque tenía muchas manchas rojas en su piel y sentía picazón por todo el cuerpo. Además, sabía que tendría que recibir algunas vacunas y tratamientos para aliviar sus síntomas.

Marta entró en la habitación de Sofía con una sonrisa cálida y le dijo: "¡Hola, Sofía! Soy Marta, tu enfermera hoy. Estoy aquí para cuidarte y asegurarme de que te sientas mejor pronto". Sofía miró a Marta con ojos preocupados y preguntó: "¿Me va a picar mucho cuando me pongan las inyecciones?".

Marta se agachó a la altura de Sofía y le explicó con ternura: "Sé que las inyecciones pueden asustar un poco, pero te prometo que serán rápidas y que estaré contigo todo el tiempo. También te traeré algo para la picazón en la piel". Sofía asintió con cautela, pareciendo un poco más tranquila.

Durante el día, Marta cuidó de Sofía, le dio medicamentos para aliviar su resfriado y aplicó loción calmante en sus manchas de varicela. También le trajo algunos libros para colorear y jugar juntas. Marta hizo todo lo posible para que Sofía se sintiera cómoda y segura.

Al final del día, Sofía sonrió y le dijo a Marta: "Gracias, enfermera Marta. No fue tan malo como pensaba. ¡Me siento mejor ahora!". Marta le acarició el cabello y respondió: "Estoy feliz de que te sientas mejor, Sofía. Siempre estamos aquí para cuidarte y hacer que te sientas lo más cómoda possible".

Questions:

1. Who is Sofia? _____
2. What were her symptoms?

   _____

3. What was she afraid of?

   _____

4. How did Marta manage it?

   _____

Translation:

Once upon a time, there was a nurse named Marta who worked in a pediatric hospital. One day, she was assigned the task of taking care of Sofia, a five-year-old girl who had been diagnosed with chickenpox and also had a common cold. Sofia was very scared because she had many red spots on her skin and she felt itchy all over her body. Additionally, she knew that she would have to receive some vaccines and treatments to alleviate her symptoms.

Marta entered Sofía's room with a warm smile and said, "Hello, Sofía! I'm Marta, your nurse today. I'm here to take care of you and make sure you feel better soon." Sofia looked at Marta with worried eyes and asked, "Will I be really itchy when they give me the injections?"

Marta crouched down to Sofia's height and explained tenderly: "I know the injections can be a little scary, but I promise they will be quick and that I will be with you the entire time. I will also bring you something for your itchy skin." Sofia nodded cautiously, seeming a little calmer.

During the day, Marta took care of Sofía, giving her medicine to relieve her cold and applying soothing lotion to her chickenpox spots. She also brought her some books to color and play with together. Marta did everything possible to make Sofía feel comfortable and safe.

At the end of the day, Sofia smiled and said to Marta, "Thank you, Nurse Marta. It wasn't as bad as she thought. I feel better now!" Marta stroked her hair and responded, "I'm happy that you feel better, Sofía. We are always here to take care of you and make you feel as comfortable as possible."

B. Complete the following sentences:

1. *Durante la _____ cardíaca, se registraron anormalidades en el ECG.*

2. *La cirugía de bypass coronario es un tratamiento común para la _____.*

3. *El marcapasos es un dispositivo utilizado para regular el ritmo _____.*

4. *El electrocardiograma es una prueba que registra la actividad _____.*

5. *El infarto de miocardio se produce cuando hay un bloqueo en una arteria _____.*

6. *La _____ puede causar dificultad para respirar y fatiga.*

7. *El paciente se sometió a un cateterismo cardíaco para evaluar la salud de sus _____.*

8. *La _____ cardíaca puede deberse a la acumulación de placa en las arterias.*

9. *La angina de pecho es un síntoma de que el corazón no recibe suficiente _____.*

Answers:

1. *Arritmia*
2. *Enfermedad cardíaca coronaria*
3. *Cardíaco*
4. *Cardíaca*
5. *Coronaria*
6. *Insuficiencia cardíaca*
7. *Arterias coronarias*
8. *Enfermedad*
9. *Oxígeno*

C. Read the following text. It's an abstract for a fictitious research. Then, read the translation:

*Exploración de las **Alteraciones Neuromotoras** en Pacientes con **Esclerosis Múltiple** mediante **Resonancia Magnética Funcional***

Resumen:

*La **esclerosis múltiple** (**EM**) es una enfermedad neurológica crónica que afecta a un número significativo de individuos en todo el mundo. Uno de los aspectos más debilitantes de la EM es la aparición de **alteraciones neuromotoras**, que pueden limitar considerablemente la movilidad y la calidad de vida de los pacientes. En este estudio, se utilizó la **resonancia magnética funcional** (**RMf**) para investigar las bases neurobiológicas de estas alteraciones en pacientes con EM. Se reclutaron veinte pacientes diagnosticados con EM y veinte participantes sanos como grupo de control. Se realizaron análisis de RMf mientras los participantes realizaban tareas motoras específicas. Los resultados revelaron **anomalías en la conectividad funcional** en regiones cerebrales clave involucradas en el control motor en los pacientes con EM en comparación con el grupo de control. Estos hallazgos proporcionan una comprensión más profunda de las **alteraciones neuromotoras** en la EM y pueden tener implicaciones importantes para el desarrollo de terapias dirigidas a mejorar la función motora en esta población de pacientes.*

Translation:

Exploration of Neuromotor Alterations in Patients with Multiple Sclerosis through Functional Magnetic Resonance Imaging

Abstract:

Multiple sclerosis (MS) is a chronic neurological disease that affects a significant number of individuals worldwide. One of the most debilitating aspects of MS is the onset of neuromotor alterations, which can significantly limit mobility and the quality of life for patients. In this study, functional magnetic resonance imaging (fMRI) was used to investigate the neurobiological basis of these alterations in patients with MS. Twenty patients diagnosed with MS and, as a control group, twenty healthy participants were recruited. fMRI analyses were conducted while participants performed specific motor tasks. The results revealed abnormalities in functional connectivity in key brain regions involved in motor control in MS patients compared to the control group. These findings provide a deeper understanding of neuromotor alterations in MS and may have important implications for the development of therapies aimed at improving motor function in this patient population.

D. Read the following conversation and complete the translation below:

HP: Buenas tardes, ¿cómo se encuentra hoy?

P: Buenas tardes, doctor. Me siento muy nerviosa y asustada.

HP: Entiendo que esto puede ser abrumador. Hemos realizado algunas pruebas y quiero hablarle sobre los resultados. Hemos detectado un tumor mamario, y es importante que comencemos el tratamiento de inmediato para evitar que se propague.

P: ¿Un tumor? ¿Qué significa eso? ¿Es cáncer?

HP: Sí, es un tumor en la mama, y debemos tratarlo con seriedad. La buena noticia es que lo hemos detectado a tiempo, y eso es crucial para el tratamiento. Quiero que sepa que estamos aquí para apoyarla en cada paso del camino.

P: ¿Qué vamos a hacer ahora?

HP: Lo primero que haremos es realizar más pruebas para determinar el tipo exacto de tumor y su extensión. Luego, trabajaremos juntos para desarrollar un plan de tratamiento personalizado que podría incluir cirugía, quimioterapia o radioterapia, dependiendo de lo que sea mejor para usted.

P: ¿Cuánto tiempo llevará el tratamiento? ¿Será doloroso?

HP: El tiempo de tratamiento varía según su caso, y trabajaremos para hacerlo lo más cómodo posible. Algunos aspectos pueden causar molestias, pero estaremos aquí para manejar cualquier síntoma que pueda experimentar. Su bienestar es nuestra principal preocupación.

P: Gracias, doctor, por ser comprensivo. Esto es aterrador, pero sé que estoy en buenas manos.

HP: Estamos aquí para usted, y juntos superaremos esto. Estaremos con usted en cada paso del camino y haremos todo lo posible para brindarle el mejor cuidado.

Translation:

HP: Good afternoon. How are you feeling today?

P: Good afternoon, doctor. I'm feeling very nervous and scared.

HP: I understand that this can be overwhelming. We have conducted some tests and I want to talk to you about the results. We have detected a _____ (1), and it's important to start treatment immediately to prevent it from spreading.

P: A tumor? What does that mean? Is it _____(2)?

HP: Yes, it's a tumor in the breast, and we must take it seriously. The good news is that we have detected it in time and that is crucial for treatment. I want you to know that we are here to support you every step of the way.

P: What are we going to do now?

HP: The first thing we will do is perform more tests to determine the exact type of tumor and its extent. Then, we will work together to develop a personalized treatment plan that could include surgery, _____(3), or _____(4), depending on what is best for you.

P: How long will the treatment take? Will it be _____(5)?

HP: The treatment time varies depending on your case, and we will work to make it as comfortable as possible. Some aspects may cause discomfort, but we will be here to manage any symptoms you may experience. Your well-being is our top concern.

P: Thank you, doctor, for being understanding. This is terrifying, but I know I'm in good hands.

HP: We are here for you, and together we will overcome this. We will be with you every step of the way and do everything we can to provide you with the best care.

Answers:

1. Breast tumor
2. Cancer
3. Chemotherapy
4. Radiation therapy
5. Painful

CROSSING THE CULTURAL BRIDGE: SENSITIVITY IN SPANISH-SPEAKING PATIENT CARE

E ffective communication in healthcare goes beyond language proficiency. It encompasses cultural awareness and sensitivity, recognizing that each patient brings a unique cultural background and perspective. This is especially evident when delivering care to Spanish-speaking patients and their families. While speaking Spanish is crucial, it's just the beginning. Understanding and respecting cultural subtleties can make a significant difference in offering patient-centered, empathetic care.

Spanish-speaking patients often come from diverse backgrounds, representing a rich variety of cultures and traditions. As healthcare professionals, your responsibility extends beyond addressing physical symptoms. It involves acknowledging and honoring the values, beliefs, and customs that influence the patient's worldview. Neglecting this cultural bridge can result in misunderstandings, hinder trust-building, and ultimately impact the quality of care.

Picture a scenario where a healthcare provider, despite being fluent in Spanish, unintentionally offends a patient by not recognizing the significance of family in their culture. Or envision a situation where a doctor prescribes treatment without considering the patient's cultural preferences and dietary restrictions, leading to non-compliance and adverse outcomes. These are just a few instances that illustrate the intricate relationship between language and culture in healthcare.

In this chapter, we will explore the cultural intricacies of Spanish-speaking patients and offer practical insights to healthcare professionals. These insights aim to ensure sensitivity and patient-focused care. By doing so, we aim to bridge the gap between language and culture, cultivating an atmosphere of trust and understanding that enriches the healthcare experience for both providers and patients.

EMBRACING CULTURAL DIVERSITY IN HEALTHCARE

Hospitals, clinics, and healthcare facilities across the globe serve a wide array of patients from various cultural backgrounds. While this diversity can indeed present challenges, it also provides an opportunity to enrich our understanding of health and wellness from different perspectives.

Studies have consistently demonstrated the profound impact of cultural sensitivity on healthcare outcomes (Krist et al., 2017). Patients who feel understood and respected by their healthcare providers are more likely to adhere to treatment plans, leading to improved health results. The converse is equally true; a lack of cultural awareness can lead to misunderstandings, patient dissatisfaction, and compromised treatment effectiveness.

One of the key takeaways from this is that a healthcare professional's ability to navigate and comprehend cultural nuances is more than just a diplomatic gesture; it is an essential aspect of delivering high-quality care. Understanding a patient's cultural background can make a significant difference in building trust and fostering effective communication.

Let's delve into a concrete example. Many Hispanic cultures have deep-rooted beliefs in holistic and natural medicine, often passed down through generations. Recognizing and respecting these beliefs is essential for healthcare professionals. It means being open to discussions about treatment options that align with these beliefs, or at the very least, acknowledging their significance in the patient's overall well-being.

For instance, a patient might express a preference for traditional herbal remedies alongside conventional medical treatment. A healthcare provider who is aware of and sensitive to these cultural preferences can engage in a productive conversation, exploring the compatibility of traditional and modern approaches to healthcare. This level of understanding goes a long way in fostering patient trust, satisfaction, and ultimately, better health outcomes.

Let the following stories be examples of how these cultural barriers can look in real-life scenarios:

- Imagine a Spanish-speaking patient, Maria, visiting a hospital for a critical consultation. The healthcare provider primarily speaks English and relies on an interpreter to communicate with Maria. While the interpreter does their best, subtle nuances and emotions in Maria's speech may be lost in translation. This gap in direct communication can lead to misunderstandings and hinder the provider's ability to fully comprehend Maria's symptoms and concerns. Moreover, Maria may feel frustrated or anxious due to her inability to express herself directly, impacting her overall experience and trust in the healthcare system.

- Juan, a Hispanic patient, has been diagnosed with a chronic illness. He believes strongly in the healing properties of herbal remedies passed down through his family for generations. When his healthcare provider suggests a treatment plan that solely relies on pharmaceutical medications, Juan feels misunderstood and resistant to the proposed approach. The provider, unaware of Juan's cultural beliefs, struggles to convince him of the benefits of modern medicine. This disconnect in understanding may lead to Juan seeking alternative treatments independently, potentially compromising his health.

These scenarios illustrate how cultural barriers, such as language differences and a lack of awareness about patients' cultural beliefs, can manifest in real-life healthcare interactions. Effective cultural competence training and open communication can help healthcare professionals overcome these barriers and provide more patient-centered care.

COMMON BELIEFS AND CUSTOMS IN SPANISH-SPEAKING CULTURES

Understanding and respecting the common beliefs and customs prevalent in Spanish-speaking cultures is vital for healthcare professionals aiming to provide culturally sensitive care. These beliefs and customs influence various aspects of patient care and can significantly impact patient satisfaction and treatment outcomes.

In many Spanish-speaking cultures, the family unit plays a central role in a person's life, including healthcare decisions. It's common for patients to involve multiple family members in discussions about their health and treatment options. Healthcare professionals should be prepared to accommodate and engage with extended family members who may accompany the patient to medical appointments. Understanding that family support is highly valued can enhance the patient-provider relationship.

Example: Carmen, a Mexican-American patient, brings her parents and siblings to her prenatal check-up. The obstetrician acknowledges and welcomes the family's presence, fostering a supportive environment.

Magical or supernatural beliefs may be a common component to mind, especially when treating older patients. The concept of "*susto*" or "fright sickness" is prevalent in many Hispanic cultures. It is believed that a sudden scare or traumatic experience can lead to physical and emotional distress. Healthcare professionals should recognize that patients may attribute their symptoms to such experiences. Understanding "*susto*" can help providers empathize with patients' concerns and respectfully explain medical conditions with their cultural beliefs.

Example: A patient, Javier, presents with unexplained anxiety and physical symptoms after witnessing a traumatic event. His therapist acknowledges the possibility of "*susto*" and incorporates trauma-informed care into the treatment plan.

On the other hand, we must address gender matters to deeply understand the Hispanic communicational dynamics. When it comes to treating Hispanic men, it's important to be aware of their cultural nuances when seeking medical advice.

"*Machismo*" refers to the traditional cultural expectation that men should be strong, stoic, and unemotional. This view influences how men perceive and express their health concerns. Men might be more reluctant to seek medical help or admit vulnerability. Healthcare professionals should be proactive in asking about symptoms and offering support, creating a safe space for male patients to discuss their health.

Example: Carlos, a Hispanic patient, experiences persistent chest pain but hesitates to seek medical attention due to the fear of appearing weak. His cardiologist engages in open dialogue, assuring him that seeking help is a sign of strength and responsibility.

Understanding and respecting these cultural nuances can bridge the gap between healthcare professionals and Spanish-speaking patients, fostering trust, effective communication, and improved healthcare outcomes.

As I previously mentioned, treating Hispanic people has its specific challenges, since their cultural background plays a role when it comes to health care. The following tips will help you navigate successfully these situations:

- Using the **patient's last name** with an appropriate title (Mr., Mrs., etc.) is a sign of respect, particularly when addressing older individuals. It acknowledges their life experience and dignity.
- Non-verbal communication, including gestures, can vary in meaning across cultures. **Being cautious with gestures** ensures that no unintended offense is taken due to cultural differences.
- It's essential to assess the clarity and cultural sensitivity of questions and instructions. **Avoid assumptions** and be prepared to **rephrase** or **provide additional context** when necessary.
- Encouraging patients to **ask questions** fosters open and transparent communication. Many patients may have concerns or require clarification but may hesitate to speak up unless prompted.
- Relying on children to translate can create awkward power dynamics within the family and may not ensure accurate communication. If the situation demands it,

it's best to use professional interpreters or language services to maintain confidentiality and accuracy.

- Be conscious of **body language** and physical contact norms. While some Hispanic cultures may have a preference for standing closer to each other while talking and using physical touch as a sign of warmth, this may not always be appropriate in a professional healthcare setting. Strike a balance between showing empathy and respecting personal and professional boundaries.

These recommendations reflect a commitment to patient-centered care and cultural competence. Healthcare professionals who follow these guidelines can enhance the patient experience and build trust with their Hispanic patients and patients from diverse backgrounds.

OVERCOMING CULTURAL BARRIERS: CASE STUDIES AND EXAMPLES

The ability to overcome cultural barriers in healthcare is a skill that healthcare professionals develop over time. Real-life case studies and examples provide valuable insights into the nuances of cultural sensitivity and how it can positively impact patient care. Here are two illustrative examples:

Imagine a Bolivian patient who attributes their illness to "*mal de ojo*" or the "evil eye," a common belief in many Hispanic cultures. Rather than dismissing this belief as superstition, a culturally sensitive healthcare professional might acknowledge the patient's concerns. They can then explain how medical treatments can be viewed as tools to "fight" the evil eye, aligning the patient's cultural belief with Western medical interventions. This approach helps the patient feel understood and respected, fostering trust and compliance with treatment recommendations.

Now, consider another scenario where a Mexican patient is diagnosed with diabetes. As traditional foods hold significant cultural and social importance in Mexican family life, instead of advising the patient to eliminate these foods entirely, a culturally sensitive approach involves discussing portion control and healthier cooking methods. The healthcare professional can work collaboratively with the patient to adapt traditional recipes to meet dietary requirements, ensuring that cultural customs remain untouched while promoting better health outcomes.

These examples emphasize the significance of understanding and respecting cultural nuances in healthcare.

Just as mastering medical vocabulary and verbal tenses is crucial, understanding and respecting cultural beliefs and customs play an indispensable role in providing effective and empathetic care, especially when treating Hispanic patients.

Our journey through cultural sensitivity has highlighted the importance of showing respect, asking questions, and being adaptable in our approach to care. We've learned that small gestures, like addressing patients by their preferred names or maintaining eye contact, can make a significant difference in building trust and rapport. We've seen that involving family members in healthcare decisions and being aware of patients' beliefs about health and illness contribute to a more patient-centered and culturally sensitive practice.

EXERCISES AND PRACTICE

A. Read the following text and answer—in Spanish—the questions below:

Me mudé a los Estados Unidos con mi hijo para estar más cerca de él y de mis nietos. Dejar mi país natal, Perú, no fue fácil; significaba dejar atrás la familiaridad de mi entorno, a mis amigos y todo lo que había conocido durante la mayor parte de mi vida. Pero la familia era mi ancla, y quería estar cerca de ellos. No sabía que este viaje me llevaría a un encuentro inesperado con la atención médica en tierras extranjeras.

A medida que pasaban los años, me adapté a mi nueva vida, pero algo no estaba bien. Un persistente y molesto dolor en la espalda comenzó a afligirme. Intenté descartarlo como el resultado natural del envejecimiento, como otros sugerían, o el resultado de una mala postura. Sin embargo, en lo más profundo de mí, sabía que había algo más en ello.

Mi hijo y mis nietos hicieron todo lo posible por cuidarme, instándome a buscar consejo médico. Estaban genuinamente preocupados por mi salud, pero yo vacilaba. Siempre había sido la que ofrecía consuelo y fuerza a mi familia, y la idea de cargarlos con mi dolor me resultaba insoportable.

Lo que no entendían era que este dolor, este peso invisible que parecía estar doblando mi espalda, era más que una dolencia física. Era el reflejo de un secreto familiar guardado durante mucho tiempo, un silencio que había llevado desde mi juventud. Sabía que este silencio, esta verdad no dicha, estaba en la raíz de mi sufrimiento.

Visitaba a varios médicos que, a pesar de sus mejores intenciones, no podían comprender la profundidad de mi angustia. Me hicieron pruebas, me sugirieron medicamentos y hasta me recomendaron fisioterapia, pero no los escuché, porque sabía—o pensaba—que ninguna de esas cosas podía aliviar mi dolor.

Entonces, un día, mientras el dolor me inmovilizaba y la desesperación amenazaba con consumirme, apareció un rayo de esperanza. Conocí al Dr. Rodríguez, un médico mexicano-americano que practicaba la medicina con una mezcla única de conocimiento occidental y sensibilidad cultural. Cuando compartí mi creencia de que mi dolor de espalda estaba relacionado con este secreto oculto, él no lo descartó ni me trató con condescendencia. En cambio, me escuchó atentamente, validando mis experiencias y emociones.

El Dr. Rodríguez reconoció que mi bienestar físico y emocional estaban entrelazados. Recomendó una cirugía de espalda para abordar el aspecto físico de mi sufrimiento y sugirió que hablara con un consejero para liberarme del secreto familiar que me había atormentado durante tanto tiempo.

Bajo el cuidado del Dr. Rodríguez, me sometí a la cirugía necesaria y, aunque la recuperación fue desafiante, mi dolor de espalda se fue reduciendo gradualmente. Al mismo tiempo, comencé mis sesiones con un consejero, desenredando el secreto arraigado que me había cargado durante décadas. No fue un viaje fácil, pero con el apoyo del Dr. Rodríguez y la orientación de mi consejero, sentí que finalmente se estaba levantando un peso pesado.

Hoy, me mantengo un poco más erguida, no solo físicamente sino también emocionalmente. He aprendido la importancia de los profesionales de la salud que no solo tratan el cuerpo, sino que también reconocen la compleja interacción entre la salud física y emocional. El enfoque compasivo y culturalmente sensible del Dr. Rodríguez me mostró el poder de la comprensión y la validación en el proceso de curación.

Translation:

I moved to the United States with my son to be closer to him and my grandchildren. Leaving my home country of Peru was not easy; it meant leaving behind the familiarity of my surroundings, my friends, and everything I had known for most of my life. But family was my anchor, and I wanted to be near them. Little did I know that this journey would lead me to an unexpected encounter with healthcare in a foreign land.

As the years passed, I settled into my new life, but something was amiss. A persistent, gnawing pain in my back began to afflict me. I tried to dismiss it as the natural result of aging, as others suggested, or the result of poor posture. However, deep down, I knew there was something more to it.

My son and my grandchildren did their best to care for me, urging me to seek medical advice. They were genuinely concerned about my health, but I hesitated. I had always been the one to offer solace and strength to my family, and the thought of burdening them with my pain felt unbearable.

What they didn't understand was that this pain, this invisible weight that seemed to be bending my back, was more than just a physical ailment. It was a reflection of a long-held family secret, a silence that I had carried since my youth. I knew that this silence, this unspoken truth, was at the root of my suffering.

I visited various doctors who, despite their best intentions, couldn't comprehend the depth of my distress. They ran tests, suggested medications, and even recommended physical therapy, but I didn't listen to them, since I knew—or thought—none of those things were able to alleviate my pain.

Then, one day, as the pain immobilized me and despair threatened to engulf me, a ray of hope appeared. I met Dr. Rodriguez, a Mexican-American doctor who practiced medicine with a unique blend of Western knowledge and cultural sensitivity. When I shared my belief that my back pain was linked to this hidden secret, he didn't dismiss it or patronize me. Instead, he listened attentively, validating my experiences and emotions.

Dr. Rodriguez recognized that my physical and emotional well-being were intertwined. He recommended back surgery to address the physical aspect of my suffering and suggested that I speak with a counselor to unburden myself of the family secret that had plagued me for so long.

Under Dr. Rodriguez's care, I underwent the necessary surgery, and though the recovery was challenging, my back pain gradually subsided. Simultaneously, I began my sessions with a counselor, unraveling the deep-rooted secret that had weighed me down for decades. It was not an easy journey, but with Dr. Rodriguez's support and the guidance of my counselor, I felt like a heavy burden was finally being lifted.

Today, I stand a little taller, not just physically but emotionally as well. I have learned the importance of healthcare professionals who not only treat the body but also recognize the complex interplay between physical and emotional health. Dr. Rodriguez's compassionate and culturally sensitive approach showed me the power of understanding and validation in the healing process.

Questions:

1. How did the protagonist's cultural background influence her reluctance to seek medical intervention?
   _____
   _____

2. What role did the Mexican-American doctor play in addressing the protagonist's health concerns?
   _____
   _____

3. In what ways did the healthcare professionals in the story demonstrate cultural sensitivity in their approach to the patient's care?
   _____
   _____

4. What were some of the cultural barriers the protagonist faced in the healthcare system?
   _____
   _____

5. How did the healthcare professionals validate the protagonist's health beliefs and experiences?
   _____
   _____

6. What was the connection between the protagonist's physical pain and her hidden family secret, as portrayed in the story?
   _____
   _____

7. What lesson can healthcare providers learn from this narrative about the importance of culturally sensitive care and communication?
   _____
   _____

Answers:

1. *La cultura de la protagonista influyó en su renuencia a buscar intervención médica, ya que tenía creencias arraigadas sobre el dolor de espalda y su relación con un secreto de familia.*
2. *El doctor mexico-americano desempeñó un papel fundamental al escuchar y validar las creencias de salud de la protagonista. Además, la convenció de someterse a una cirugía de espalda necesaria y buscar asesoramiento para liberarse del peso de su secreto familiar.*
3. *Los profesionales de la salud en la historia demostraron sensibilidad cultural al respetar y comprender las creencias de salud de la paciente, en lugar de descartarlas.*
4. *La protagonista enfrentó barreras culturales en el sistema de atención médica cuando otros médicos intentaron convencerla de que sus creencias estaban equivocadas y que su dolor de espalda tenía otras causas.*
5. *Los profesionales de la salud validaron las creencias y experiencias de salud de la protagonista al reconocer que su dolor de espalda estaba relacionado con su secreto familiar y al ofrecer soluciones que se alineaban con sus creencias.*
6. *La conexión entre el dolor físico de la protagonista y su secreto familiar radicaba en la creencia de que guardar el secreto estaba causando el dolor. La liberación del secreto a través del asesoramiento se consideró una parte crucial de su proceso de curación.*
7. *La lección que los proveedores de atención médica pueden aprender de esta narrativa es la importancia de brindar atención y comunicación culturalmente sensibles. Es vital*

escuchar y respetar las creencias y experiencias de salud de los pacientes para proporcionar un cuidado más efectivo y compasivo.

Answers Translation:

1. The protagonist's culture influenced her reluctance to seek medical intervention, as she had deep-rooted beliefs about back pain and its relationship to a family secret.
2. The Mexican-American doctor played a key role in listening to and validating the protagonist's health beliefs. Additionally, he convinced her to undergo necessary back surgery and seek counseling to free herself from the weight of her family secret.
3. Health professionals in the story demonstrated cultural sensitivity by respecting and understanding the patient's health beliefs, rather than dismissing them.
4. The protagonist faced cultural barriers in the health care system when other doctors tried to convince her that her beliefs were wrong and that her back pain had other causes.
5. The health professionals validated the protagonist's health beliefs and experiences by recognizing that her back pain was related to her family history and by offering solutions that aligned with her beliefs.
6. The connection between the protagonist's physical pain and her family's secret lies in the belief that keeping the secret was causing the pain. Releasing the secret

through her counseling was considered a crucial part of her healing process.

7. The lesson healthcare providers can learn from this narrative is the importance of providing culturally sensitive care and communication. It is vital to listen to and respect patients' health beliefs and experiences to provide more effective and compassionate care.

6

MASTERING THE INTRICACIES OF MEDICAL SPANISH

This chapter takes us deeper into the world of medical Spanish, where mastery of intricate grammar rules and complex medical terminologies becomes essential. This chapter is designed to equip healthcare professionals with the advanced language skills required to navigate intricate medical scenarios, ensuring accurate communication with Spanish-speaking patients. From the intricacies of grammar to the precision of medical terminology, the following pages provide practical insights and guidance for those committed to delivering the highest level of care to their diverse patient populations.

¡Vamos a ello!

ESCALATING YOUR GRAMMAR: THE SUBJUNCTIVE MOOD

The Spanish language is renowned for its rich grammatical features, and one of the most intricate aspects is the subjunctive mood. In medical contexts, understanding and utilizing the subjunctive mood is vital for healthcare professionals seeking to communicate with precision and nuance. This mood is often employed to express various states of unreality, including doubt, possibility, necessity, and actions that have not yet occurred. Let's delve into how the subjunctive mood functions in Spanish and how it can enhance communication with Spanish-speaking patients.

In the realm of healthcare, expressing necessity and making recommendations are daily occurrences. The subjunctive mood is particularly valuable in these scenarios. For instance, consider the phrase "*Es importante que el paciente tome su medicamento,*" which translates to "It's important that the patient takes his medication." In this context, the subjunctive mood conveys a sense of necessity. The healthcare professional is emphasizing the importance of the patient taking their prescribed medication for their well-being.

Beyond necessity, the subjunctive mood is also employed to express wishes and give advice. For instance, you might encounter the phrase "*Es mejor que descanses,*" which can be translated as "It is better if you rest." In this case, the use of the subjunctive mood signifies that resting is advisable for the patient's benefit. It offers a gentle and caring way to make recommendations, acknowledging that the patient has agency in the decision.

Understanding the subtleties of the subjunctive mood in Spanish can significantly enhance communication with Spanish-speaking patients, especially in situations where advice, recommendations, or possible treatment outcomes need to be conveyed. When healthcare professionals can navigate the subjunctive mood effectively, they not only communicate medical information accurately but also demonstrate a level of linguistic proficiency that fosters trust and rapport with their patients.

So, let's start by analyzing the conjugation of the verb *"ser"* (to be) in the present subjunctive for the grammatical personals that we learned back in Chapter 1:

Pronoun	Conjugation (ser)
Yo	*sea*
Tú	*seas*
Él/Ella/Usted	*sea*
Nosotros	*seamos*
Vosotros	*seáis*
Ellos/Ellas/Ustedes	*sean*

Examples:

- *Es fundamental que el médico sea comprensivo y respetuoso al tratar a los pacientes de diferentes culturas.*

- (It is essential that the doctor be understanding and respectful when treating patients from different cultures.)
- *Recomiendo que ustedes **sean** conscientes de las creencias culturales de sus pacientes para brindarles una atención más sensible.*
- (I recommend that you all be aware of your patient's cultural beliefs to provide more sensitive care.)
- *Es importante que los profesionales de la salud **seamos** capaces de comunicarnos efectivamente en español médico para garantizar un cuidado de calidad.*
- (It is important that healthcare professionals be capable of communicating effectively in medical Spanish to ensure quality care.)

Here's a chart with the conjugations of the verb "*estar*" (to be) in the past, present, and future simple subjunctive tenses:

Subject pronoun	Past simple subjunctive	Present simple subjunctive	Future simple subjunctive
Yo	estuviera	esté	estuviere
Tú	estuvieras	estés	estuvieres
Él/Ella/Usted	estuviera	esté	estuviere
Nosotros(as)	estuviéramos	estemos	estuviéremos
Vosotros(as)	estuvierais	estéis	estuviereis
Ellos/Ellas/Ustedes	estuvieran	estén	estuvieren

Examples:

- *Quería que él **estuviera** en la reunión.* (I wanted him to be at the meeting.) -Past simple subjunctive.
- *Es importante que tú **estés** tranquilo.* (It's important that you are calm.) -Present simple subjunctive.
- *Si no vienen, llamaré a un familiar para que **estuviere** presente.* (If they don't come, I will call a relative so that they will be present.) -Future simple subjunctive.

As we previously mentioned, the present subjunctive tense in Spanish is a valuable tool for healthcare professionals when they need to express advice and recommendations or discuss possible treatment outcomes. This tense allows for more nuanced communication, conveying necessity, doubt, or possibility. Let's explore this further with examples and charts featuring the conjugations of the verbs "***tener***" (to have) and "***necesitar***" (to need) in the present subjunctive.

The present subjunctive of "***tener***" can be used to express the necessity of something. For example:

- *Es importante que el paciente **tenga** una dieta equilibrada.* (It's important that the patient has a balanced diet.)
- *El médico recomienda que ustedes **tengan** cuidado con el sol.* (The doctor recommends that you all be careful with the sun.)

Here's the chart with the conjugations of "***tener***" in the present subjunctive:

Pronoun	Conjugation
Yo	tenga
Tú	tengas
Él/Ella/Usted	tenga
Nosotros(as)	tengamos
Vosotros(as)	tengáis
Ellos/Ellas/ Ustedes	tengan

The present subjunctive of "*necesitar*" can be used to discuss the patient's need for specific treatments or care. For example:

- *No creo que el paciente **necesite** que el médico le dé una receta.* (I don't think the patient needs the doctor to give them a prescription.)
- *Es probable que **necesitemos** hacer un examen de orina.* (We may need to do a urine test.)

Here's the chart with the conjugations of "*necesitar*" in the present subjunctive:

Pronoun	Conjugation
Yo	necesite
Tú	necesites
Él/Ella/Usted	necesite
Nosotros(as)	necesitemos
Vosotros(as)	necesitéis
Ellos/Ellas/Ustedes	necesiten

NAVIGATING COMPOUND TENSES

In Spanish, compound tenses are a crucial aspect of effective communication, especially when discussing healthcare matters. These tenses are used to indicate actions that have a specific relationship with other actions in terms of time and completion. Understanding and using compound tenses correctly can greatly enhance your ability to convey complex medical information to Spanish-speaking patients.

The **compound past perfect** tense is frequently used in healthcare conversations to describe actions that have occurred in the past and are still relevant to the present moment. It is formed by combining the auxiliary verb "*haber*" (to have) with the past participle of the main verb. Here's an example:

- "*El paciente **ha** tomado su medicamento*" (The patient **has** taken his medication).

In this sentence, "*ha tomado*" (has taken) is in the past perfect tense. It indicates that the action of taking medication happened at some point in the past, and its effects or relevance continues into the present. This tense is valuable when discussing a patient's recent medical history, ensuring that you convey the continuity of their actions or treatments.

The **compound future perfect** tense is used to express the assumption or speculation that an action will have been completed by a specific future time or event. This tense can be particularly useful when discussing treatment plans, expected outcomes, or predictions related to a patient's health. It is formed by combining the future tense of the auxiliary verb "***haber***" with the past participle of the main verb. Here's an example:

- "*El paciente **habrá** terminado su tratamiento en un mes*" (The patient **will** have finished his treatment in a month).

In this sentence, "*habrá terminado*" (will have finished) is in the future perfect tense. It suggests that, based on current information or planning, the patient's treatment is expected to be completed in the future. This can help healthcare professionals communicate effectively about long-term treatment goals and anticipated results.

Mastering compound tenses in Spanish allows healthcare professionals to convey intricate medical information with precision and clarity. For example, you can use the past perfect tense to describe a patient's detailed medical history, providing a comprehensive understanding of their prior health conditions and treatments. On the other hand, the future perfect tense enables you to discuss treatment plans and expected outcomes, giving patients a clear picture of what lies ahead in their healthcare journey.

Here's a chart that conjugates the verb "*ser*" in the past and future compound tenses in Spanish, along with sentences related to a clinical environment using each tense:

Verb "ser" (to be)	Past perfect tense	Future perfect tense
Yo	he sido	habré sido
Tú	has sido	habrás sido
Él/Ella/Usted	ha sido	habrá sido
Nosotros(as)	hemos sido	habremos sido
Vosotros(as)	habéis sido	habréis sido
Ellos/Ellas/Ustedes	han sido	habrán sido

Examples:

- *En el pasado, el paciente **ha** sido muy activo antes de su lesión.* (In the past, the patient has been very active before his injury). -Compound past perfect
- *Hasta el momento, el diagnóstico **ha** sido ambiguo, pero seguiremos investigando.* (So far, the diagnosis has been ambiguous, but we will continue investigating). - Compound past perfect

- *Para la próxima cita, el paciente **habrá** sido sometido a una serie de pruebas adicionales.* (By the next appointment, the patient will have undergone a series of additional tests). -Compound future perfect

Let's see other verbs conjugated in the **compound past perfect** tense:

Pronouns	Verb "tomar" (to take)	Verb "descansar" (to rest)	Verb "recuperar" (to recover)
Yo	he tomado	he descansado	he recuperado
Tú	has tomado	has descansado	has recuperado
Él/Ella/Usted	ha tomado	ha descansado	ha recuperado
Nosotros(as)	hemos tomado	hemos descansado	hemos recuperado
Vosotros(as)	habéis tomado	habéis descansado	habéis recuperado
Ellos/Ellas/Ustedes	han tomado	han descansado	han recuperado

Examples:

- Yo **he** *tomado* la temperatura del paciente cada dos horas. (I have taken the patient's temperature every two hours).
- El médico pregunta si el paciente **ha** *descansado* al menos ocho horas antes de la cirugía. (The doctor asks if the patient has rested at least eight hours before surgery).

- Después de la operación, el paciente **ha** *recuperado* la conciencia gradualmente. (After the surgery, the patient has gradually regained consciousness).

It can be challenging to differentiate between a compound tense and another. Here's a chart with the pronouns and the conjugation for the past and future compound tenses for the verb "***necesitar***" (to need) so you can better notice the difference. Don't forget to check the use examples below:

Pronouns	Past perfect (I had needed)	Future perfect (I will have needed)
Yo	he necesitado	habré necesitado
Tú	has necesitado	habrás necesitado
Él/Ella/Usted	ha necesitado	habrá necesitado
Nosotros(as)	hemos necesitado	habremos necesitado
Vosotros(as)	habéis necesitado	habréis necesitado
Ellos/Ellas/Ustedes	han necesitado	habrán necesitado

Examples:

- *Antes de la cirugía, el paciente **ha** necesitado tomar medicamentos para reducir el dolor.* (Before the surgery, the patient had needed to take medication to reduce the pain). -Compound past perfect
- *Durante su recuperación, el paciente **ha** necesitado atención médica constante.* (During their recovery, the patient had needed constant medical care). -Compound past perfect

- *Después de la cirugía, el paciente **habrá** necesitado tiempo para descansar y recuperarse por completo.* (After the surgery, the patient will have needed time to rest and fully recover). -Compound future perfect

DECODING IDIOMATIC EXPRESSIONS

Idiomatic expressions, known as *"expresiones idiomáticas"* in Spanish, are phrases that carry a figurative meaning that is often different from their literal translation. They are a distinctive feature of the Spanish language and are used extensively in everyday conversations. Understanding these expressions is crucial for effective communication, especially in a healthcare setting.

Being aware of these expressions is essential for healthcare professionals when interacting with Spanish-speaking patients. These expressions often carry nuanced meanings that can significantly affect the context of a conversation. Here's how understanding idiomatic expressions can enhance patient communication:

- Misinterpreting idiomatic expressions can lead to misunderstandings in healthcare discussions. For example, if a patient says, *"Me duele el brazo, pero no es la gran cosa"* (My arm hurts, but it's not the big thing), they might downplay their symptoms.
- Familiarity with idiomatic expressions can foster a stronger rapport with Spanish-speaking patients. When healthcare professionals acknowledge and use these

expressions appropriately, it conveys a level of cultural competence and empathy. Patients may feel more comfortable and understood when their healthcare provider recognizes and responds to their use of idiomatic language.

Here are some of the most common idiomatic expressions in Spanish, along with their meanings:

- *"Estar en las nubes:"* To be daydreaming or not paying attention, often used when someone is mentally distracted.
- *"Más sano que una pera:"* To be in very good health, indicating robust well-being.
- *"Echar agua al mar:"* To do something pointless or futile, similar to "casting pearls before swine."
- *"Costar un ojo de la cara:"* To cost an arm and a leg, indicating something is very expensive.
- *"Estar en las últimas:"* To be on one's last legs, typically referring to someone who is very ill or exhausted.
- *"Meter la pata:"* To put one's foot in one's mouth or make a big mistake.
- *"Dar en el clavo:"* To hit the nail on the head, meaning to be exactly right about something.
- *"Ser pan comido:"* To be a piece of cake, indicating that something is very easy.
- *"Tener mala leche:"* To be in a bad mood or have a bad attitude.
- *"Estar en el séptimo cielo:"* To be in seventh heaven, signifying extreme happiness or bliss.

- *"Buscarle la quinta pata al gato:"* To look for trouble where there isn't any, similar to "making a mountain out of a molehill."

ADVANCED MEDICAL TERMINOLOGIES

In this section, we will explore a wide range of complex medical terms in Spanish. You'll encounter specific illnesses and conditions, as well as advanced medical procedures and treatments. These terms are essential for healthcare professionals who want to provide precise and accurate information to Spanish-speaking patients. Understanding these advanced medical terminologies will enable you to navigate intricate medical discussions and offer comprehensive care.

Here is a chart with common diseases and chronic conditions encountered in healthcare settings, along with their translations and pronunciation in Spanish:

English term	Spanish translation	Pronunciation
Anemia	Anemia	ah-neh-mee-ah
Asthma Attack	Ataque de asma	ah-tah-keh deh ahs-mah
Celiac Disease	Enfermedad celíaca	ehn-fehr-meh-dahd seh-lee-ah-kah
Chronic Obstructive Pulmonary Disease (COPD)	Enfermedad Pulmonar Obstructiva Crónica (EPOC)	ehn-fer-meh-dahd pool-moh-nahr ohbs-troock-tee-vah kroh-nee-kah
Glaucoma	Glaucoma	glaw-koh-mah
Hepatitis	Hepatitis	eh-pah-tee-tees
High Cholesterol	Colesterol alto	koh-leh-ste-rol al-toh
Hemorrhoids	Hemorroides	eh-moh-roy-dehs
Hypoglycemia	Hipoglucemia	ee-poh-gloo-seh-mee-ah
Hypothyroidism	Hipotiroidismo	ee-poh-tee-roh-ee-dees-moh
Kidney Stones	Cálculos renales	kahl-koo-lohs reh-nah-lehs
Lupus	Lupus	loo-poos
Multiple Sclerosis	Esclerosis Múltiple	ehs-kleh-roh-sees mool-tee-pleh
Osteoarthritis	Osteoartritis	ohs-teh-oh-ar-tree-teess
Osteosarcoma	Osteosarcoma	ohs-teh-oh-sar-koh-mah
Parkinson's Disease	Enfermedad de Parkinson	ehn-fehr-meh-dahd deh pahr-keen-sohn
Psoriasis	Psoriasis	soh-ree-ah-sis
Rheumatoid Arthritis	Artritis reumatoide	ahr-tree-teess reh-oo-mah-tow-ee-deh
Tuberculosis	Tuberculosis	too-ber-koo-loh-sis
Varicose Veins	Venas varicosas	veh-nahs vah-ree-koh-sahs

Next, here is the chart with the medical equipment terms:

English term	Spanish translation	Pronunciation
Ambulance	Ambulancia	ahm-boo-lahn-syah
Bedpan	Orinal	oh-ree-nahl
Blood Bag	Bolsa de sangre	bohl-sah deh sahn-greh
Blood Pressure Monitor	Monitor de presión arterial	moh-nee-tor deh preh-see-on ahr-teh-ryahl
Crutches	Muletas	moo-leh-tahs
Defibrillator	Desfibrilador	des-fee-bree-lah-dohr
EKG Machine	Máquina de electrocardiograma	mah-kee-nah deh eh-lehk-troh-kar-dee-oh-grah-mah
Electrocardiogram (ECG) Machine	Máquina de electrocardiograma (ECG)	mah-kee-nah deh eh-lehk-troh-kar-dee-oh-grah-mah
Electroencephalogram (EEG) Machine	Máquina de electroencefalograma (EEG)	mah-kee-nah deh eh-lehk-troh-en-sef-ah-loh-grah-mah
Echocardiogram (Echo) Machine	Máquina de ecocardiograma (Echo)	mah-kee-nah deh eh-koh-kar-dee-oh-grah-mah
Glucometer	Glucómetro	gloo-koh-meh-tro
IV (Intravenous) Drip	Goteo intravenoso	goh-teh-oh een-trah-veh-noh-soh
IV Catheter	Catéter intravenoso	kah-teh-tehr een-trah-veh-noh-soh
IV Pole	Soporte para suero	soh-por-teh pah-rah sweh-roh
MRI Machine	Máquina de resonancia magnética	mah-kee-nah deh reh-soh-nahn-see-ah mahg-neh-tee-kah
Nebulizer	Nebulizador	neh-boo-lee-sah-dor
Ophthalmoscope	Oftalmoscopio	ohf-tahl-moh-sko-pee-oh
Otoscope	Otoscopio	oh-toh-sko-pee-oh
Pulse Oximeter	Oxímetro de pulso	ok-see-meh-tro deh pool-soh
Scales	Báscula	bahs-koo-lah
Scalpel	Bisturí	bee-stoo-ree

Sphygmomanometer	Esfigmomanómetro	es-feeg-moh-mah-noh-meh-tro
Stethoscope	Estetoscopio	ehs-teh-tohs-koh-pee-oh
Suction Machine	Máquina de succión	mah-kee-nah deh sook-see-ohn
Surgical Gloves	Guantes quirúrgicos	gwahn-tehs kee-roor-hee-kohs
Thermometer	Termómetro	ter-moh-meh-tro
Tourniquet	Torniquete	tohr-nee-ket-eh
Ultrasound Machine	Máquina de ultrasonido	mah-kee-nah deh ool-trah-soh-nee-doh
Ventilator	Ventilador	ven-tee-lah-dor
Wheelchair	Silla de ruedas	see-yah deh roo-eh-dahs
X-ray Machine	Máquina de rayos X	mah-kee-nah deh rah-yos eh-kees

These terms are now sorted alphabetically to facilitate easy reference for healthcare professionals working with Spanish-speaking patients.

Examples:

- El paciente fue diagnosticado con diabetes, **por lo que necesita llevar un** glucómetro *para controlar su nivel de azúcar en la sangre.* (The patient was diagnosed with diabetes, so he needs to carry a glucometer to monitor his blood sugar level.)
- *La paciente sufrió una lesión grave y se realizó una* **resonancia magnética** *para evaluar el alcance de los daños en su columna vertebral.* (The patient suffered a serious injury, and an MRI was performed to assess the extent of damage to her spine.)
- *Después de la cirugía, se le colocó un* **catéter intravenoso** *para administrar los medicamentos de manera continua.*

(After surgery, an IV catheter was placed to administer medications continuously.)

- *El paciente experimenta una* **hipertensión** *persistente que requiere medicación para controlar su presión arterial alta.* (The patient experiences persistent hypertension that requires medication to control his high blood pressure.)

- *La* **radiografía** *mostró una fractura en el húmero, lo que explicaría el dolor intenso en el brazo.* (The X-ray revealed a fracture in the humerus, which would explain the intense pain in the arm.)

- *La* **cirugía laparoscópica** *se realizó con éxito para extirpar el* **apéndice inflamado** *y aliviar los síntomas del paciente.* (The laparoscopic surgery was performed successfully to remove the inflamed appendix and relieve the patient's symptoms.)

EXERCISES AND PRACTICE

A. Use the present perfect subjunctive of the verb "*ver*" (to see) to fill in the blanks:

1. *El médico insiste en que el paciente no _____ (ver) más sangrado.*
2. (The doctor insists that the patient doesn't see any more bleeding.)
3. *Espero que tú _____ (ver) mejoras en tu salud pronto.*
4. (I hope that you see improvements in your health soon.)

Answers:

1. *vea*
2. *veas*

B. Complete the sentences using the present perfect subjunctive of "*entender*" (to understand):

1. *Es fundamental que los profesionales de la salud* _____ *(entender) las necesidades de los pacientes.*
2. (It is essential that healthcare professionals understand the patients' needs.)
3. *Dudo que el padre*_____ *(entender) la gravedad de la situación.*
4. (I doubt that the father understands the seriousness of the situation.)

Answers:

1. *entiendan*
2. *entienda*

C. Consider the conjugation of the verb "*haber*" (to have) in the present perfect subjunctive and complete the sentences below:

Pronoun	Conjugation (present subjunctive)
Yo	haya
Tú	hayas
Él/Ella	haya
Nosotros/Nosotras	hayamos
Vosotros/Vosotras	hayáis
Ellos/Ellas	hayan

1. *Quiero que tú _____(1) entendido las instrucciones.* (I want you to have understood the instructions.)
2. *Es necesario que él _____(2) completado el tratamiento.* (It is necessary for him to have completed the treatment.)
3. *Espero que ustedes _____(3) tomado la medicina a tiempo.* (I hope that you all have taken the medicine on time.)

Answers:

1. *hayas*
2. *haya*
3. *hayan*

D. Consider the conjugation of the verb "*saber*" (to know) in the past, present, and future simple subjunctive tenses and complete the sentences below:

1. *Es importante que tú* _____ *la respuesta correcta* (present subjunctive of "*saber*").
2. *Quería que él* _____ *la verdad* (past subjunctive of "*saber*").
3. *Es crucial que ellos* _____ *qué hacer en caso de emergencia* (present subjunctive of "*saber*").

Answers:

1. *Sepas*
2. *Supiera/supiese*
3. *Sepan*

E. Read the following dialogue and identify the compound tenses of the bold verbs:

Doctor (D): *Buenos días, señor García. Veo que* **ha** *tenido (1) algunos síntomas preocupantes recientemente.* _____

Paciente (P): *Sí, doctor.* **He** *sentido (2) fatiga y dolores en el pecho.* _____

D: *Comprendo su preocupación. Primero,* **ha** *tenido (3) problemas cardíacos en el pasado, ¿verdad?* _____

P: *Sí, tuve un infarto hace algunos años.*

D: *Entiendo. Hemos realizado algunos estudios y* **ha** *salido (4) un poco de irregularidad en su ritmo cardíaco. Esto podría estar relacionado con su historial médico.* _____

P: *¿Qué debo hacer al respecto, doctor?*

*D: Para su diagnóstico, **hemos** decidido hacer (5) un electrocardio-grama adicional y le recomendamos realizarlo lo antes posible. Esto nos permitirá entender mejor su situación.*

_____

P: Está bien, doctor. ¿Y cuál es el tratamiento?

*D: Una vez tengamos los resultados, **habremos** determinado (6) la mejor opción de tratamiento para usted. Deberá seguir una dieta y un régimen de ejercicios específicos, además de **haber** tomado (7) medica-mentos para controlar su ritmo cardíaco.*

_____, _____

*P: Gracias, doctor. **Habré** seguido (8) sus instrucciones al pie de la letra. _____*

D: Eso es muy importante, señor García. Estamos aquí para ayudarlo a mejorar su salud y calidad de vida.

Answers:

1. Past perfect
2. Past perfect
3. Past perfect
4. Past perfect
5. Past perfect
6. Future perfect
7. Future perfect
8. Future perfect

Translation:

D: Good morning, Mr. García. I see that you've *experienced* (1) some concerning symptoms recently.

P: Yes, doctor. I've *felt* (2) fatigue and chest pains.

D: I understand your concern. First, you've *had* (3) heart problems in the past, correct?

P: Yes, I had a heart attack a few years ago.

D: I understand. We've conducted some tests, and there **has** *been* (4) a bit of irregularity in your heart rhythm. This could be related to your medical history.

P: What should I do about it, doctor?

D: For your diagnosis, we've *decided* to perform (5) an additional electrocardiogram, and we recommend that you have it done as soon as possible. This will allow us to better understand your situation.

P: Alright, doctor. And what is the treatment?

D: Once we have the results, we **will have** *determined* (6) the best treatment option for you. You'll need to follow a specific diet and exercise regimen, in addition to **having** *taken* (7) medications to control your heart rhythm.

P: Thank you, doctor. I **will have** *followed* (8) your instructions to the letter.

D: That's very important, Mr. García. We're here to help you improve your health and quality of life.

7

CONVERSING SPANISH: A CAREER CATALYST

In the final chapter of our journey through the world of medical Spanish, we delve into a realm beyond the clinical setting. While the previous chapters equipped you with the linguistic skills and cultural insights necessary for providing exceptional patient care, this chapter unveils a new dimension: how mastering Spanish can elevate your healthcare career.

We explore how your proficiency in Spanish can be a career catalyst, opening doors to new opportunities and enhancing your professional profile. In a world that increasingly values cultural diversity and effective communication, your ability to converse in Spanish can be a valuable asset.

LANGUAGE SKILLS AS A CAREER BOOSTER

Being bilingual is an incredible asset in today's interconnected world, and when it comes to the healthcare industry, this proficiency becomes even more valuable. In this chapter, we explore the myriad opportunities that mastering Spanish can unlock in the healthcare sector. From improved earning potential to enhanced patient-provider relationships, your ability to converse in Spanish can truly be a career catalyst.

One of the most compelling reasons to embrace bilingualism, especially in a language as widely spoken as Spanish, is the economic advantage it brings. According to a study, bilingual workers tend to earn between 5% to 20% more per hour than their monolingual counterparts (Shin & Alba, 2009). This wage premium is a testament to the high demand for bilingual professionals across various industries, including healthcare.

In the realm of healthcare, where effective communication is paramount, bilingual healthcare professionals are sought after. Hospitals, clinics, and medical practices often prioritize candidates who can bridge language gaps and connect with diverse patient populations. This not only opens doors to higher-paying positions but also contributes to greater job satisfaction.

The ability to communicate with a larger patient population broadens your career horizons in healthcare. In an increasingly diverse society, healthcare providers must cater to patients from various cultural and linguistic backgrounds. Your proficiency in Spanish allows you to serve as a crucial link between healthcare services and Spanish-speaking patients.

Beyond the clinical setting, your language skills can be a valuable asset in administrative roles, healthcare management, or public health initiatives that target Spanish-speaking communities.

Effective communication is at the heart of quality healthcare, and being bilingual can significantly enhance the patient-provider relationship. When patients can communicate directly with their healthcare providers in their preferred language, it fosters trust and rapport.

Moreover, bilingual healthcare professionals can offer a more personalized and efficient healthcare experience. Eliminating the need for interpreters streamlines the communication process, reducing the risk of miscommunication and ensuring that crucial medical information is accurately conveyed.

Your Spanish language skills are a valuable asset that should be prominently featured on your resume. When applying for healthcare positions, whether as a nurse, physician, pharmacist, or any other role, consider including your language proficiency in the "skills" section of your CV.

For instance, you might write, "proficient in medical Spanish, with experience providing healthcare to Spanish-speaking patients." This concise statement immediately communicates your ability to interact with a diverse patient population and can capture the attention of potential employers.

During job interviews, take the opportunity to showcase how your Spanish skills have positively impacted your work. Share specific examples of how effective communication in Spanish has led to improved patient care, better outcomes, or enhanced collaboration with colleagues.

If you've undergone formal training or hold certifications in Spanish language proficiency, such as those from the American

Council on the Teaching of Foreign Languages (ACTFL), be sure to include them on your resume. Certifications provide tangible evidence of your language proficiency and can set you apart from other candidates.

Additionally, certifications from reputable organizations like ACTFL are widely recognized and respected in the industry. They demonstrate your commitment to maintaining high language standards and can be a powerful endorsement of your language skills.

Building strong relationships with colleagues and patients is crucial in healthcare. Embracing Spanish in your professional interactions can be a meaningful way to connect with Spanish-speaking colleagues and foster a more inclusive workplace environment.

Simple gestures like greeting your Spanish-speaking colleagues in their native language can go a long way in building camaraderie and showing respect for their culture. Engaging in casual conversations or using Spanish during team meetings can help strengthen bonds and create a more cohesive healthcare team.

Furthermore, attending networking events or professional conferences specifically designed for Spanish-speaking healthcare professionals can be a game-changer for your career. These events provide a unique platform to practice your Spanish language skills, exchange insights with peers, and expand your professional network.

As you progress in your career, it's essential to continue expanding your medical vocabulary in Spanish. In previous chapters, we've explored the fundamentals of medical Spanish, from basic conversational phrases to specialized terminology. Now, let's dive deeper into the expansive world of Spanish medical terminology, where precision in communication is paramount.

Healthcare is a field rich in specialized terminology. Whether you work in primary care, surgery, pediatrics, or any other specialty, you'll encounter a myriad of medical terms specific to your area of expertise. These terms often require an in-depth understanding, not only of their meanings but also of their correct pronunciation and usage.

For example, consider the difference between "*osteoporosis*" and "*osteomalacia*." While both terms involve bone health, they represent distinct conditions with unique characteristics and treatment approaches. Mastery of such nuances is essential for accurate diagnosis and treatment.

CONTINUOUS LEARNING AND IMPROVEMENT

As a healthcare professional, the journey of mastering Spanish is a lifelong commitment. In this final section, we will explore strategies for continuous learning and improvement in Spanish, as well as turning challenges into opportunities for growth.

- Language proficiency, like any skill, requires regular practice. Embracing technology can make this easier than ever. Language learning apps such as Babbel or Rosetta Stone offer specialized courses in medical Spanish. These apps provide structured lessons and interactive exercises, allowing you to practice medical terminology and conversational skills at your own pace. Consistent practice is key to retaining and enhancing your language skills.

- Staying informed about the latest developments in your field is essential for any healthcare professional. Consider reading medical journals or articles in Spanish to expand your vocabulary and stay up-to-date with medical advancements. Websites like Medscape Español offer a wealth of medical content in Spanish. Reading specialized articles can help you grasp complex medical terminology and improve your comprehension.

- Engaging in conversation is one of the most effective ways to improve your language skills. Look for Spanish language clubs or conversation groups in your local community. Opt for groups that include other healthcare professionals so that you can practice medical Spanish within a relevant context. These interactions not only enhance your language proficiency but also provide a supportive community of like-minded individuals.

- Learning medical terminology can be challenging, but it's a hurdle that can be overcome with focused practice. If you struggle with recalling specific medical terms, consider creating flashcards. Write the medical term in

Spanish on one side and its English translation on the other. Regularly reviewing these flashcards can help reinforce your memory and improve your ability to recall medical vocabulary accurately.

- Understanding the cultural nuances of your Spanish-speaking patients can be a complex task. Healthcare professionals often find it challenging to navigate the cultural differences that may impact patient care. However, this challenge can be turned into an opportunity for growth. Consider taking a course in Hispanic culture or healthcare in Hispanic communities. These courses not only deepen your cultural awareness but also equip you with valuable insights into patient expectations, beliefs, and behaviors.

- Finding time for language learning can be difficult, especially for busy healthcare professionals. However, integrating Spanish into your daily routine can make it more manageable. Utilize your commute time by listening to Spanish podcasts related to healthcare or general conversation. During breaks or downtime at work, practice speaking Spanish with colleagues who are also eager to improve their language skills. These small but consistent efforts can add up to significant progress over time.

In conclusion, mastering Spanish as a healthcare professional is an ongoing journey that requires dedication and commitment. By following these strategies for continuous learning and addressing challenges as opportunities for growth, you can enhance your language skills, provide more effective patient care, and open doors to new career opportunities. Remember that language proficiency is not a destination but a continuous process of improvement, enriching both your professional and personal life.

CONCLUSION

As we reach the end of this extensive guide, it's essential to recap the key points and encourage you, the dedicated healthcare hero, to continue your Spanish learning journey.

Throughout this book, we've explored the critical role that Spanish proficiency plays in the healthcare industry. We started with the basics, laying a strong foundation by delving into Spanish grammar rules, essential vocabulary, and common medical terminologies. We then progressed to practical applications, providing you with scenarios where your newfound Spanish skills could make a significant difference in patient care.

We ventured into specialized vocabulary tailored to different healthcare fields, ensuring that you're well-equipped to communicate effectively in your specific area of expertise. We also delved into the cultural nuances of Spanish-speaking patients, emphasizing the importance of sensitivity and patient-centered care.

For those seeking to take their Spanish skills to the next level, we delved into advanced grammar rules and complex medical terminologies, preparing you for more intricate conversations and challenging scenarios.

Our journey has highlighted the benefits of learning Spanish in the healthcare industry. By mastering this language, you unlock the ability to communicate seamlessly with Spanish-speaking patients, grasp common medical terms, and apply your knowledge practically.

Remember that the ultimate purpose of this book is to empower you to break down language barriers, enhance your communication skills, and provide the best possible care to your patients. You have embarked on a path that not only enriches your professional life but also impacts the lives of those you serve.

As we conclude, I encourage you to continue honing your Spanish skills. Consider delving further into your language journey by exploring my previous book, *Learn Spanish for Adult Beginners: Speak Confidently & Impress Your Amigos. A No-Nonsense Guide to Quickly Learn Vocabulary, Common Phrases and Master Pronunciation* (Mancilla, 2023), where you can build upon your foundational knowledge and become fluent beyond the clinical setting.

Apply what you've learned in your interactions with Spanish-speaking patients. Utilize additional resources, such as language learning apps or engaging with Spanish-speaking colleagues, for continued practice and learning.

If you found this essential guide to Spanish for healthcare professionals beneficial, I would greatly appreciate your feedback. Sharing your thoughts and experiences through reviews can be a valuable way to support fellow language learners and healthcare heroes. Your review will serve as an inspiration and encouragement for others embarking on their journey to speak Spanish confidently.

Please scan the QR code below to leave your review.

Your commitment to learning Spanish is a testament to your dedication to patient care and professional growth. Embrace this journey as an enriching experience that will positively impact your career and the lives of those you serve.

Thank you for joining me on this adventure of language and healthcare. I wish you continued success, fulfillment, and satisfaction in your healthcare profession.

Gracias por tu compromiso y empatía con las personas hispanohablantes.

¡Adelante y éxito en su viaje de aprendizaje del español!

APPENDIX

In this section, you will find exercises, dialogues, more vocabulary, and grammar reinforcements to continue practicing your Spanish and take it to the next level. Take your time doing the exercises and try not to consult the answers unless necessary or to double-check.

Have fun learning this wonderful language!

A. Complete the following sentences with the appropriate definite article (el, la, los, or las) in Spanish:

1. _____ *obstetra examina a la paciente.* (masculine)
2. _____ *bebés nacieron sanos.* (masculine)
3. _____ *parto fue complicado pero exitoso.*
4. _____ *enfermeros están cuidando a las pacientes.*
5. _____ *ginecólogo brinda atención especializada.*
6. _____ *mujeres embarazadas necesitan controles regulares.*

7. _____ *cirujano realizó una cesárea.*

8. _____ *pacientes están en la sala de espera.*
   (femenine)

9. _____ *recién nacido está en perfecto estado.*

10. _____ *parteras ayudaron en el parto en casa.*

11. _____ *ecografía reveló el género del bebé.*

12. _____ *pacientes deben seguir las indicaciones*
    médicas.

13. _____ *anestesista administró la epidural.*
    (masculine)

14. _____ *madres primerizas a veces tienen ansiedad.*

15. _____ *médico realiza exámenes de rutina.*

Translation:

1. The obstetrician examines the patient.
2. The babies were born healthy.
3. The childbirth was challenging but successful.
4. The nurses are taking care of the patients.
5. The gynecologist provides specialized care.
6. Pregnant women need regular check-ups.
7. The surgeon performed a cesarean section.
8. The patients are in the waiting room.
9. The newborn is in perfect condition.
10. The midwives assisted with the home birth.
11. The ultrasound revealed the baby's gender.
12. Patients must follow medical instructions.
13. The anesthesiologist administered the epidural.
14. First-time mothers sometimes experience anxiety.
15. The doctor conducts routine exams.

Answers:

1. *El*
2. *Los*
3. *El*
4. *Los*
5. *El*
6. *Las*
7. *El*
8. *Las*
9. *El*
10. *Las*
11. *La*
12. *Los*
13. *El*
14. *Las*
15. *El*

B. Fill in the blanks with the appropriate personal pronouns (yo, tú, él, ella, nosotros, vosotros, ellos, ellas) in Spanish:

1. _____ *soy el anestesiólogo encargado de la cirugía.*
2. _____ *debes administrar la anestesia de manera precisa.*
3. _____ *tiene experiencia en anestesiología pediátrica.*
4. _____ *estudia las reacciones a los anestésicos.*
5. _____ *trabajamos en equipo en el quirófano.*
6. _____ *debéis estar preparados para emergencias.*
7. _____ *investigan nuevas técnicas anestésicas.*
8. _____ *cuidan a los pacientes antes de la cirugía.*

9. _____ *explicaré el procedimiento a la paciente.*

10. _____ *monitorizas constantemente la presión arterial.*

11. _____ *debe calcular la dosis adecuada del anestésico.*

12. _____ *prefiere la anestesia regional.*

13. _____ *nos preocupamos por el bienestar del paciente.*

14. _____ *tenéis experiencia en anestesia obstétrica.*

15. _____ *acompañan al paciente a la sala de recuperación.*

Answers:

1. *Yo*
2. *Tú*
3. *Él/Ella*
4. *Él/Ella*
5. *Nosotros/as*
6. *Vosotros/as*
7. *Ellos/Ellas*
8. *Ellos/Ellas*
9. *Yo*
10. *Tú*
11. *Él/Ella*
12. *Él/Ella*
13. *Nosotros/as*
14. *Vosotros/as*
15. *Ellos/Ellas*

Translation:

1. I am the anesthesiologist in charge of the surgery.
2. You must administer anesthesia accurately.
3. He/She has experience in pediatric anesthesiology.
4. He/She studies reactions to anesthetics.
5. We work as a team in the operating room.
6. You all must be prepared for emergencies.
7. They research new anesthesia techniques.
8. They take care of patients before surgery.
9. I will explain the procedure to the patient.
10. You continuously monitor blood pressure.
11. He/She must calculate the appropriate dose of the anesthetic.
12. He/She prefers regional anesthesia.
13. We care about the patient's well-being.
14. You all have experience in obstetric anesthesia.
15. They accompany the patient to the recovery room.

C. Complete the following sentences by conjugating the given verbs in the specified tense (present simple, past perfect simple, or future simple) in Spanish:

1. (*Hablar*; Presente Simple) *El paciente _____ con el terapeuta sobre sus preocupaciones.*
2. (*Comprender*; Pasado Perfecto Simple) *El psicólogo _____ las razones detrás de su ansiedad.*
3. (*Resolver*; Futuro Simple) *El tratamiento _____ los problemas emocionales del paciente.*

4. (*Analizar*; Presente Simple) *Los expertos* _____ *los síntomas del trastorno.*

5. (*Superar*; Pasado Perfecto Simple) *El paciente* _____ *sus traumas pasados.*

6. (*Evaluar*; Futuro Simple) *El psiquiatra* _____ *el progreso del tratamiento.*

7. (*Observar*; Presente Simple) *Los investigadores* _____ *el comportamiento del grupo de control.*

8. (*Diagnosticar*; Pasado Perfecto Simple) *El médico* _____ *el trastorno en una etapa temprana.*

9. (*Mejorar*; Futuro Simple) *La terapia* _____ *la calidad de vida del paciente.*

10. (*Tratar*; Presente Simple) *Los profesionales* _____ *a personas con trastornos mentales.*

11. (*Entender*; Pasado Perfecto Simple) *Ella* _____ *la causa de su depresión.*

12. (*Prevenir*; Futuro Simple) *La medida* _____ *futuros episodios de ansiedad.*

13. (*Diagnosticar*; Presente Simple) *Los especialistas* _____ *trastornos neuropsiquiátricos.*

14. (*Controlar*; Pasado Perfecto Simple) *El paciente* _____ *sus impulsos agresivos.*

15. (*Guiar*; Futuro Simple) *El terapeuta* _____ *al paciente hacia la recuperación.*

Answers:

1. *Habla*
2. *Comprendió*
3. *Resolverá*

4. *Analizan*

5. *Superó*

6. *Evaluará*

7. *Observan*

8. *Diagnosticó*

9. *Mejorará*

10. *Tratan*

11. *Entendió*

12. *Prevenirá*

13. *Diagnostican*

14. *Controló*

15. *Guiará*

Translation:

1. The patient speaks with the therapist about their concerns.
2. The psychologist understood the reasons behind their anxiety.
3. The treatment will resolve the patient's emotional issues.
4. The experts analyze the symptoms of the disorder.
5. The patient overcame his/her past trauma.
6. The psychiatrist will evaluate the progress of the treatment.
7. The researchers observe the behavior of the control group.
8. The doctor diagnosed the disorder at an early stage.
9. The therapy will improve the patient's quality of life.
10. Professionals treat people with mental disorders.

11. She understood the cause of her depression.

12. The measure will prevent future episodes of anxiety.

13. Specialists diagnose neuropsychiatric disorders.

14. The patient controlled his aggressive impulses.

15. The therapist will guide the patient toward recovery.

D. Look at the bold verbs and identify in which tense and for which grammatical person they are conjugated:

*Cirujano (C): Buenos días, doctor. Tenemos a la paciente García en la sala de operaciones. **Prepararon**(1) todo el equipo necesario para la cirugía de reconstrucción de la fractura de fémur.*

*Anestesiólogo (A): Buenos días, doctor. Me **alegra**(2) escuchar eso. Antes de proceder, ¿**ha revisado**(3) la historia clínica de la paciente?*

*C: Sí, la **revisé**(4). La paciente **sufrió**(5) un accidente en moto hace tres días y **presentó**(6) múltiples fracturas. Su estado general **ha sido**(7) estable hasta el momento, pero **necesitamos**(8) realizar esta cirugía para evitar complicaciones a largo plazo.*

*A: Entiendo. ¿La paciente **ha recibido**(9) algún tipo de medicación preoperatoria?*

*C: No, aún no. **Hablé**(10) con ella antes de la cirugía para asegurarme de que no **comió**(11) alimentos ni tomó líquidos en las últimas ocho horas, como se recomienda.*

*A: Perfecto. **Voy**(12) a administrar la anestesia general. Una vez que la paciente esté dormida, ¿cuánto tiempo **durará**(13) la cirugía?*

*C: Estimamos que la cirugía **llevará**(14) aproximadamente tres horas. Durante ese tiempo, **debemos**(15) realizar la reducción de la fractura y fijar la placa y los tornillos para asegurar la estabilidad del hueso.*

*A: Entendido, doctor. Me **aseguraré**(16) de mantener a la paciente bajo anestesia de manera segura durante todo el procedimiento.*

*C: Excelente. Una vez que **haya finalizado**(17) la cirugía, **necesitaremos**(18) su colaboración para despertar a la paciente y monitorizar su recuperación en la sala de recuperación postoperatoria.*

*A: Por supuesto, **estaré**(19) allí para supervisar la transición de la paciente del estado de sedación al de conciencia. Después **continuaremos**(20) evaluando su estado y administrando el manejo del dolor según sea necesario.*

Translation:

Surgeon (S): Good morning, doctor. We have patient García in the operating room. They prepared all the necessary equipment for the femur fracture reconstruction surgery.

Anesthesiologist (A): Good morning, doctor. I'm glad to hear that. Before proceeding, have you reviewed(3) the patient's medical history?

S: Yes, I reviewed it. The patient suffered a motorcycle accident three days ago and she presented multiple fractures. Her general condition has been stable, but we need to perform this surgery to avoid long-term complications.

A: I understand. Has the patient received any preoperative medication?

S: No, not yet. I spoke with her before surgery to make sure she did not eat or drink in the last eight hours, as recommended.

A: Oh, perfect. I am going to administer general anesthesia. Once the patient is asleep, how long will the surgery last?

S: We estimate that the surgery will take approximately three hours. During that time, we must perform fracture reduction and fix the plate and screws to ensure the stability of the bone.

A: Understood, doctor. I will make sure to keep the patient safely under anesthesia throughout the procedure.

S: Excellent. Once the surgery has been completed, we will need your collaboration to wake up the patient and monitor her recovery in the post-operative recovery room.

A: Of course, I will be there to supervise the patient's transition from anesthesia to consciousness. Afterward, we will continue to assess her condition and administer pain management as necessary.

Answers:

[Infinitive verb]: *[tense]*; *[Personal pronoun]*

1. **Preparar**: *Pasado perfecto simple; Ellos/as*
2. **Alegrar**: *Presente; Yo*
3. **Revisar**: *Pasado perfecto compuesto; Usted*
4. **Revisar**: *Pasado perfecto simple; Yo*
5. **Sufrir**: *Pasado perfecto simple; Ella*
6. **Presentar**: *Pasado perfecto simple; Ella*
7. **Ser**: *Pasado perfecto compuesto; Ella*

8. *Necesitar:* Presente; Nosotros/as
9. **Recibir:** Pasado perfecto compuesto; Ella
10. **Hablar:** Pasado perfecto simple; Yo
11. **Comer:** Pasado perfecto simple; Ella
12. **Ir:** Presente; Yo
13. **Durar:** Futuro Simple; Ella (la cirugía)
14. **Llevar:** Futuro Simple; Ella (la cirugía)
15. **Deber:** Presente; Nosotros/as
16. **Asegurar:** Futuro Simple; Yo
17. **Finalizar:** Pasado perfecto compuesto; Ella (la cirugía)
18. **Necesitar:** Futuro Simple; Nosotros/as
19. **Estar:** Futuro Simple; Yo
20. **Continuar:** Futuro Simple; Nosotros/as

E. Read the following dialogue and translate the bold words:

Niño (N): ¡Hola, doctor! **Mamá**(1) me dijo que necesito **anteojos**(2) porque tengo **miopía**(3) y **astigmatismo**(4), pero no entiendo qué significa eso. ¿Puede explicármelo?

Oftalmólogo (O): ¡Hola! Claro que puedo explicártelo. La miopía y el astigmatismo son dos **problemas de la visión**(5). Comencemos por la miopía. La miopía significa que puedes ver claramente los **objetos cercanos**(6), como un libro, pero tienes **dificultades**(7) para ver **cosas lejanas**(8), como la pizarra en la escuela.

N: Ah, entiendo. ¿Y qué es el astigmatismo?

O: Bueno, el astigmatismo es un poco diferente. En el astigmatismo, la forma de tu **ojo**(9) no es perfectamente **redonda**(10), como una pelota. En cambio, puede ser más como un balón de rugby. Esto hace que la luz que entra en tu ojo no se **enfoque**(11) adecuadamente en un solo punto de la **retina**(12), y eso provoca **visión borrosa**(13) tanto de cerca como de lejos.

N: Gracias, doctor. ¿Cómo saben que tengo estos problemas? ¿Qué hacen en la **consulta**(14)?

O: Para saber si tienes miopía y astigmatismo, te haremos un **examen visual completo**(15). Usaremos una máquina llamada **refrac-tómetro**(16) para medir la forma en que la luz se dobla cuando pasa por tu ojo. También puedes mirar a través de una serie de **lentes**(17) mientras lees **letras**(18) en una **carta de Snellen**(19) para determinar cuál te ayuda a ver más claramente.

N: ¿Y los anteojos ayudarán a que pueda ver mejor?

O: Exacto, los anteojos corregirán estos problemas. Para la miopía, los lentes tendrán una forma específica para ayudar a que los rayos de luz se enfoquen adecuadamente en tu retina, permitiéndote ver objetos lejanos con claridad. En el caso del astigmatismo, los lentes serán especialmente diseñados para enderezar la luz y mejorar tu visión tanto de cerca como de lejos.

N: Gracias por explicármelo, doctor. ¿Cómo serán los anteojos?

O: Los anteojos serán diseñados para que se adapten a tu **prescrip-ción**(20) exacta. Pueden ser de diferentes estilos y colores, ¡así que podrás elegir los que más te gusten!

Answers:

1. Mom
2. Glasses
3. Myopia

4. Astigmatism
5. Vision problems
6. Near objects
7. Difficulties
8. Distant objects
9. Eye
10. Round
11. Focus
12. Retina
13. Blurry vision
14. Consultation
15. Comprehensive visual examination
16. Refractometer
17. Lenses
18. Letters
19. Snellen chart
20. Prescription

Translation:

Child (C): Hello, doctor! Mom told me I need glasses because I have myopia and astigmatism, but I don't understand what that means. Can you explain it to me?

Ophthalmologist (O): Hello! Of course, I can explain it to you. Myopia and astigmatism are two vision problems. Let's start with myopia. Myopia means that you can see objects up close, like a book, clearly, but you have difficulties seeing distant things, like the chalkboard at school.

C: Ah, I see. And what is astigmatism?

O: Well, astigmatism is a bit different. In astigmatism, the shape of your eye is not perfectly round, like a ball. Instead, it can be more like a rugby ball. This causes the light entering your eye not to focus properly on a single point of the retina, and that causes blurry vision both up close and far away.

C: Thank you, doctor. How do they know I have these problems? What do they do during the consultation?

O: To find out if you have myopia and astigmatism, we will perform a comprehensive visual examination. We will use a machine called a refractometer to measure how light bends when it passes through your eye. You will also look through a series of lenses while reading letters on a Snellen chart to determine which one helps you see more clearly.

C: Will glasses help me see better?

O: Exactly. Glasses will correct these problems. For myopia, the lenses will have a specific shape to help the light rays focus properly on your retina, allowing you to see distant objects clearly. In the case of astigmatism, the lenses will be specially designed to straighten the light and improve your vision both up close and far away.

C: Thank you for explaining it, doctor. What will the glasses look like?

O: The glasses will be designed to fit your exact prescription. They can come in different styles and colors, so you can choose the ones you like the most!

F. Read the following scenarios and write down (in Spanish) below what you would do as a healthcare professional:

Escenario 1: *Un paciente en la sala de emergencias presenta síntomas de un infarto de miocardio, como dolor en el pecho intenso y opresión.*

_____

_____

Escenario 2: *Una mujer embarazada llega al hospital con contracciones regulares y fuertes.*

_____

_____

Escenario 3: *En la unidad de cuidados intensivos, un paciente está experimentando una crisis epiléptica.*

_____

_____

Escenario 4: *Un niño es traído a la sala de urgencias con una fiebre alta y dificultad para respirar.*

_____

_____

Escenario 5: *Un paciente mayor es admitido en el hospital con síntomas de un posible derrame cerebral.*

_____

_____

Translation:

Scenario 1: A patient in the emergency room presents with symptoms of a heart attack, such as severe chest pain and tightness.

Scenario 2: A pregnant woman arrives at the hospital with regular, strong contractions.

Scenario 3: In the intensive care unit, a patient is experiencing a seizure.

Scenario 4: A child is brought to the emergency room with a high fever and difficulty breathing.

Scenario 5: An elderly patient is admitted to the hospital with symptoms of a possible stroke.

Potential Answers:

1. *Debes tomar medidas rápidas para estabilizar al paciente, administrar aspirina y preparar para una posible angioplastia.* (You must take quick measures to stabilize the patient, administer aspirin, and prepare for possible angioplasty.)

2. *Como profesional de la salud, debes evaluar su estado y ayudar en el proceso de parto, brindando apoyo y monitorizando al bebé y a la madre.* (As a health professional, you must evaluate her condition and help in the birth process, providing support and monitoring the baby and the mother.)

3. *Tu tarea es administrar medicamentos antiepilépticos y tomar medidas para evitar lesiones durante la convulsión.* (Your task is to administer antiepileptic medications and take steps to prevent injury during the seizure.)

4. *Como profesional de la salud, debes realizar una evaluación completa, tomar muestras para pruebas y administrar tratamiento para la enfermedad respiratoria.* (As a healthcare professional, you must perform a complete evaluation, collect samples for testing, and administer treatment for the respiratory illness.)

5. *Tu responsabilidad es realizar una evaluación neurológica rápida, tomar una tomografía computarizada cerebral y*

administrar tratamiento para minimizar el daño cerebral. (Your responsibility is to perform a quick neurological evaluation, take a brain CT scan, and administer treatment to minimize brain damage.)

G. Observe the following diagram and match the diagnosis with the appropriate treatment:

Diagnósticos:

1. *El paciente presenta síntomas de fiebre alta, dolor de garganta y fatiga. Tras un examen físico y análisis de sangre, se confirma que padece una infección viral aguda. No se observan signos de infección bacteriana.*
2. *Este paciente tiene antecedentes de alergias estacionales y presenta síntomas de congestión nasal, picazón en los ojos y estornudos frecuentes. Después de una evaluación clínica, se confirma una reacción alérgica.*
3. *El paciente ha experimentado dolor abdominal, diarrea y fiebre durante varios días. Después de exámenes de laboratorio y una revisión completa de la historia médica, se establece el diagnóstico de gastroenteritis bacteriana.*

Tratamientos:

A.

- *Reposo en cama para permitir que el cuerpo se recupere.*
- *Hidratación constante con agua, caldos claros y bebidas electrolíticas.*

- *Antibióticos recetados específicos para tratar la infección bacteriana.*
- *Evitar alimentos grasos, picantes y lácteos hasta que los síntomas mejoren.*

B.

- *Descanso absoluto en casa.*
- *Hidratación adecuada con agua y bebidas isotónicas.*
- *Analgésicos de venta libre para reducir la fiebre y aliviar el dolor de garganta.*
- *Evitar el contacto cercano con otras personas para prevenir la propagación de la infección.*

C.

- *Antihistamínicos de venta libre para aliviar la congestión nasal y la picazón en los ojos.*
- *Uso de un humidificador en el dormitorio para mantener la humedad adecuada.*
- *Evitar la exposición a alérgenos conocidos, como el polen.*
- *Consulta de seguimiento si los síntomas persisten o empeoran.*

Answers:

1-B

2-C

3-A

Translations:

Diagnosis:

1. The patient presents symptoms of high fever, sore throat, and fatigue. After a physical examination and blood tests, it is confirmed that he suffers from an acute viral infection. No signs of bacterial infection are observed.
2. This patient has a history of seasonal allergies and presents with symptoms of nasal congestion, itchy eyes, and frequent sneezing. After clinical evaluation, an allergic reaction is confirmed.
3. The patient has experienced abdominal pain, diarrhea, and fever for several days. After laboratory tests and a complete review of the medical history, the diagnosis of bacterial gastroenteritis is established.

Treatments:

A.

- Bed rest to allow the body to recover.
- Constant hydration with water, clear broths, and electrolyte drinks.
- Specifically prescribed antibiotics to treat the bacterial infection.
- Avoid fatty, spicy, and dairy foods until symptoms improve.

B.

- Absolute rest at home.
- Adequate hydration with water and isotonic drinks.
- Over-the-counter pain relievers to reduce fever and relieve sore throat.
- Avoid close contact with other people to prevent the spread of infection.

C.

- Over-the-counter antihistamines to relieve nasal congestion and itchy eyes.
- Using a humidifier in the bedroom to maintain proper humidity.
- Avoid exposure to known allergens, such as pollen.
- Follow-up visit if symptoms persist or worsen.

H. Read the following text where a healthcare professional communicates her diagnosis to an oncological patient compassionately and efficiently, and answer (in Spanish) the questions below:

Juana, antes que nada, quiero que sepas que estamos aquí para apoyarte en cada paso de este camino. Comprendemos que este es un momento difícil para ti y estamos comprometidos a brindarte la mejor atención posible. Quiero comenzar explicándote tu diagnóstico y el plan de tratamiento que hemos diseñado para ti.

Después de realizar una serie de pruebas y análisis médicos, hemos confirmado que tienes un Linfoma no Hodgkin en estadio III. Este es un tipo de cáncer que afecta el sistema linfático, que es parte fundamental de tu sistema inmunológico. La buena noticia es que hemos identificado esto a tiempo, y con el tratamiento adecuado, tenemos la esperanza de controlar y tratar tu enfermedad de manera efectiva.

El plan de tratamiento que hemos propuesto para ti es una combinación de quimioterapia e inmunoterapia, seguida de radioterapia. La quimioterapia se utiliza para eliminar las células cancerosas en tu cuerpo y reducir el tamaño del tumor. La inmunoterapia, por otro lado, es una terapia más específica que estimula tu sistema inmunológico para que pueda reconocer y atacar las células cancerosas de manera más efectiva. La radioterapia se utilizará después de la quimioterapia e inmunoterapia para tratar áreas específicas donde el cáncer pueda persistir.

Sabemos que esta información puede ser abrumadora, pero estamos aquí para responder a todas tus preguntas y preocupaciones. Estas a salvo con nosotros.

Questions:

1. *¿Cuál es el diagnóstico médico de Juana?* (What is Juana's medical diagnosis?)
   _____
   _____

2. *¿Cuál es el objetivo de la quimioterapia en el plan de tratamiento?* (What is the goal of chemotherapy in the treatment plan?)
   _____
   _____

3. *¿Qué función tiene la inmunoterapia en el tratamiento de Juana?* (What is the role of immunotherapy in Juana's treatment?)
   _____
   _____

4. *¿Cuándo se utilizará la radioterapia en el plan de tratamiento?* (When will radiation therapy be used in the treatment plan?)
   _____
   _____

5. *¿Qué se enfatiza en cuanto a la comunicación con Juana durante esta conversación?* (What is emphasized regarding communication with Juana during this conversation?)
   _____
   _____

Translation of the text:

Juana, first of all, I want you to know that we are here to support you every step of the way. We understand that this is a difficult time for you and we are committed to providing you with the best care possible. I want to start by explaining your diagnosis and the treatment plan we have designed for you.

After performing a series of tests and medical analyses, we have confirmed that you have stage III non-Hodgkin lymphoma. This is a type of cancer that affects the lymphatic system, which is a fundamental part of your immune system. The good news is that we have identified this early, and with the right treatment, we hope to control and treat your disease effectively.

The treatment plan we have proposed for you is a combination of chemotherapy and immunotherapy, followed by radiotherapy. Chemotherapy is used to kill cancer cells in your body and shrink the tumor. Immunotherapy, on the other hand, is a more specific therapy that stimulates your immune system so it can recognize and attack cancer cells more effectively. Radiation therapy will be used after chemotherapy and immunotherapy to treat specific areas where cancer may persist.

We know this information can be overwhelming, but we are here to answer all your questions and concerns. You are safe with us.

I. Observe and learn the following vocabulary about hours of the day and days of the week and their proper usage when prescribing medication to patients:

Horas del día (Hours of the day)

- 12:00 a.m. - *Medianoche*
- 1:00 a.m. - *La una de la madrugada*
- 2:00 a.m. - *Las dos de la madrugada*
- 3:00 a.m. - *Las tres de la madrugada*
- 4:00 a.m. - *Las cuatro de la madrugada*
- 5:00 a.m. - *Las cinco de la madrugada*
- 6:00 a.m. - *Las seis de la mañana*
- 7:00 a.m. - *Las siete de la mañana*
- 8:00 a.m. - *Las ocho de la mañana*
- 9:00 a.m. - *Las nueve de la mañana*

- 10:00 a.m. - *Las diez de la mañana*
- 11:00 a.m. - *Las once de la mañana*
- 12:00 p.m. - *El mediodía*
- 1:00 p.m. - *La una de la tarde*
- 2:00 p.m. - *Las dos de la tarde*
- 3:00 p.m. - *Las tres de la tarde*
- 4:00 p.m. - *Las cuatro de la tarde*
- 5:00 p.m. - *Las cinco de la tarde*
- 6:00 p.m. - *Las seis de la tarde*
- 7:00 p.m. - *Las siete de la noche*
- 8:00 p.m. - *Las ocho de la noche*
- 9:00 p.m. - *Las nueve de la noche*
- 10:00 p.m. - *Las diez de la noche*
- 11:00 p.m. - *Las once de la noche*

Now, let's include some non-o'clock times:

- 1:30 a.m. - *La una y media de la madrugada*
- 2:45 a.m. - *Las dos y cuarenta y cinco de la madrugada*
- 3:15 a.m. - *Las tres y quince de la madrugada*
- 4:20 a.m. - *Las cuatro y veinte de la madrugada*
- 5:45 a.m. - *Las cinco y cuarenta y cinco de la madrugada*
- 6:10 a.m. - *Las seis y diez de la mañana*
- 7:55 a.m. - *Las siete y cincuenta y cinco de la mañana*
- 8:45 a.m. - *Las ocho y cuarenta y cinco de la mañana*
- 9:30 a.m. - *Las nueve y treinta de la mañana*
- 10:15 a.m. - *Las diez y quince de la mañana*
- 1:45 p.m. - *La una y cuarenta y cinco de la tarde*
- 2:20 p.m. - *Las dos y veinte de la tarde*
- 3:50 p.m. - *Las tres y cincuenta de la tarde*

- 4:40 p.m. - *Las cuatro y cuarenta de la tarde*
- 5:25 p.m. - *Las cinco y veinticinco de la tarde*
- 6:05 p.m. - *Las seis y cinco de la tarde*
- 7:30 p.m. - *Las siete y treinta de la noche*
- 8:15 p.m. - *Las ocho y quince de la noche*
- 9:50 p.m. - *Las nueve y cincuenta de la noche*

Días de la semana (Days of the week)

- *Lunes*: Monday
- *Martes*: Tuesday
- *Miércoles*: Wednesday
- *Jueves*: Thursday
- *Viernes*: Friday
- *Sábado*: Saturday
- *Domingo*: Sunday

Examples of use:

- *Le recomiendo tomar este medicamento todos los días a las 8 de la mañana para controlar su presión arterial, comenzando el lunes próximo.* (I recommend taking this medication every day at 8 a.m. to control your blood pressure, starting next Monday.)
- *Los martes y jueves, a las 6 de la tarde, asegúrese de hacer ejercicio moderado durante 30 minutos para fortalecer su sistema cardiovascular.* (On Tuesdays and Thursdays at 6 p.m., be sure to do moderate exercise for 30 minutes to strengthen your cardiovascular system.)

- *A partir del miércoles, tome una pastilla antes de cada comida principal, es decir, a las 8 de la mañana, 1 de la tarde y 7 de la noche.* (Starting Wednesday, take one pill before each main meal, that is, at 8 a.m., 1 p.m. and 7 p.m.)

- *Durante todo el fin de semana, desde el viernes hasta el domingo, recuerde descansar lo suficiente y tomar abundante líquido para ayudar en la recuperación.* (Throughout the weekend, from Friday to Sunday, remember to get plenty of rest and drink plenty of fluids to aid recovery.)

- *El próximo lunes, a las 10 de la mañana, acuda a nuestra clínica para realizar un seguimiento y ajustar su plan de tratamiento según sea necesario.* (Next Monday at 10 a.m., come to our clinic to follow up and adjust your treatment plan as needed.)

REFERENCES

Colon, I. (2019). *New research examines the economic benefits of bilingualism.* New America. http://newamerica.org/education-policy/edcentral/new-research-examines-economic-benefits-bilingualism/

Dzulkifli, M. A., & Mustafar, M. F. (2013). The influence of color on memory performance: A review. *The Malaysian Journal of Medical Sciences: MJMS, 20*(2), 3–9. https://www.ncbi.nlm.nih.gov/pmc/articles/PMC3743993/

Krist, A. H., Tong, S. T., Aycock, R. A., & Longo, D. R. (2017). Engaging patients in decision-making and behavior change to promote prevention. *Studies in Health Technology and Informatics, 240*(240), 284–302. https://www.ncbi.nlm.nih.gov/pmc/articles/PMC6996004/

Mancilla, S. (2023, July 8). *Learn Spanish for adult beginners: Speak confidently & impress your amigos. A no-nonsense guide to quickly learn vocabulary, common phrases and master pronunciation.*

Martinez, G. (2015). *Spanish in the U.S. Health Delivery System.* Instituto Cervantez | Harvard University.

McCarthy, N. (2020, December 11). *Infographic: The world's most spoken languages.* Statista Infographics. https://www.statista.com/chart/12868/the-worlds-most-spoken-languages/

Lown, B. (n.d.). *Dr. Bernard Lown.* Lown Institute. https://lowninstitute.org/about/dr-bernard-lown/

Shin, H.-J., & Alba, R. (2009). The economic value of bilingualism for Asians and Hispanics. *Sociological Forum, 24*(2), 254–275. https://www.jstor.org/stable/40210401

Thompson, S. (2021, May 27). *The U.S. has the second-largest population of spanish speakers—how to equip your brand to serve them.* Forbes. https://www.forbes.com/sites/soniathompson/2021/05/27/the-us-has-the-second-largest-population-of-spanish-speakers-how-to-equip-your-brand-to-serve-them/

www.ingramcontent.com/pod-product-compliance
Lightning Source LLC
Chambersburg PA
CBHW030257130626
46549CB00002B/565